FROM TOBACCO TO TECHNOLOGY

Reshaping Winston-Salem
for the 21st Century

"Never doubt that a small group of thoughtful, committed citizens can change the world. Indeed, it is the only thing that ever has."
Margaret Mead

This is a story of perseverance. Of what one committed individual can do over several decades by bringing together other committed people to change the economic fiber of their community.

From the beginning, Doug Maynard was concerned that the demise of manufacturing and corporate headquarters – so prevalent during the 1970s – would mean the demise of Winston-Salem – the city that he loved.

Driven by the desire to ensure that his city remained a thought and business leader – a place where people wanted to come and wanted to stay – he set out to find a new future and a new economy. No one knew what to do and, in the beginning, many doubted that Winston-Salem could become a center of technology and a host for a research park. Indeed, many of his colleagues at the medical center were not involved in economic development or applied research – their expertise was research, not commercialization.

Doug wasn't sure what to do, but he knew he had to do something, and he was pretty sure there were opportunities connected to the medical community. With the backing of the Chamber of Commerce, he went to work. Time and time again his spirits were buoyed and then plummeted as the chosen course proved not to be viable. But he never gave up.

"Sometimes I would get down," he reflected, "and we would go out to visit Archie Davis in his home." Mr. Davis had been the founder of the Research Triangle Park who, early on, had counseled Doug to keep persisting, saying it had taken 25 years for RTP to be successful. "The one thing Mr. Davis made clear in those afternoons we sat in his living room was that our vision was worth fighting for, and that we would succeed, even though it would take time."

Riding around Pinetree Golf Course in one of the more optimistic moments, Doug and I imagined a sprawling suburban research park that would unite the Triad community and even selected the location for the office building where we both would have an office to get away from our daily work and work on creating the Piedmont Triad Research Park. Alas, that was just one dream that was not to be.

As the years wore on with modest successes and many, many failures, Doug kept on. During the times, when he needed someone's influence or expertise he found them and persuaded them to lend their support. Some disappeared as things didn't pan out the way everyone expected. But a small group of committed individuals kept on, discarding one path when it no longer was viable; then trying another and another and another; making a little bit of progress at a time. For nearly two decades they persevered – riding out the highs and lows; celebrating the wins – always optimistic that things were going to take off on their own; mourning the losses; and then getting right back to work on an alternate plan.

"If there's one message in all of this," Doug once said, "it's perseverance. Having a vision is one thing. Having the fortitude to carry on despite setback after setback – to never lose sight of the vision but to be willing to go down another path – to settle temporarily for the possible instead of holding out for the ideal – that is the message here. I hope that people will remember that success did not come easily and honor the people who worked to give Winston-Salem a chance for a new future."

A modest man, Doug shunned taking any of the credit and refused to be a spokesperson out front for the work. The metal sculpture, "Triple Helix," in the Wake Forest Innovation Quarter, which was dedicated to him in 2003, had to be commissioned and installed in secret because we knew he would insist it not be dedicated to him but to all the people who had worked on the effort for so many years. The plaque on the sculpture thanks Doug Maynard for his "outstanding service to Wake Forest and the community of greater Winston-Salem," adding that he "laid the foundation on which the park is built."

Harry Truman famously said, "It is amazing what you can accomplish if you do not care who gets the credit." There's nothing more fitting to describe this modest man. In fact, he cared very much that others got the credit for all that he did.

Gayle Anderson

Contents

FOREWORD

A crucial principle of life is this: the ability to adapt is the ability to survive. The survival and development of communities most often is dependent on their ability to adapt to forces both internal and external.

Evolution, on the other hand, occurs over time, a slow but steady change, often unseen but immensely powerful in its outcome.

And so it has been with our city. Compare the Winston-Salem of the early 1990s to the Winston-Salem of today, and the changes are staggering. In a city once dominated by tobacco, banking, and textiles, innovation has emerged as the driver of a new knowledge-based economy. Nowhere is this more evident than in the Wake Forest Innovation Quarter, and at no time has that adaptation been more pronounced than in recent years.

Since 2012, we have witnessed the opening of numerous inspirational workplaces in Innovation Quarter: Wake Forest Biotech Place; 635 Vine Street – the new headquarters for Inmar; the multi-tenant 525@Vine building; the Center for Design Innovation; and the 60s Series Buildings – home to the new Bowman Gray Center for Medical Education of the Wake Forest School of Medicine and the new undergraduate programs for Wake Forest University in biomedical science and engineering. Installed infrastructure includes fiber optic cabling, Research Parkway and its link to U.S. 52, a storm-water retention system, and several parking developments. Underway is the repurposing of Bailey Power Plant – with its iconic chimney stacks – into a mixed-use facility for innovation, retail, and entertainment, plus a large residential complex to include

I

markets and restaurants.

This rapid growth is contributing to the vibrancy of downtown Winston-Salem with its new hotels, restaurants, and living and office spaces.

The drumbeat of progress is evident. Today, the Innovation Quarter is home to more than 60 companies employing about 3,300 workers in high-tech fields such as biomedicine, information technology, advanced materials, digital media, and services companies. Upwards of 6,000 students, ranging from workforce trainees to graduate and medical students, attend here. And those numbers are all continuing to grow.

But the Innovation Quarter is more than a place. It is more than a collection of numbers. This is a story about people. People who, in the words of David Bowie, "hear the future coming" and work tirelessly to equip our city with the resources and infrastructure to meet that future.

The Innovation Quarter is also the story of an evolution within an evolution. What was conceived as a 12-acre urban research park has grown into a 145-acre district for innovation. The traditional model of a drive-in, drive-out research park was poorly equipped to handle the realities of 21st century place-making. By embracing the lifestyle demands of today's knowledge workers, the Innovation Quarter is committed to a trajectory that embraces not only the creation of research facilities, but also spaces and places where the people who come here can work, live, learn, and play. The Innovation Quarter will soon have 1,200 residences within or adjacent to its edges including the recently opened Plant 64, the Gallery Lofts, Winston Factory Lofts, and the Residences at Reynolds Building, and soon the Link Apartments and additional apartments in Goler Heights. The newly created Bailey Park acts as a vibrant meeting point for a diverse set of community activities ranging from concerts to networking events to cycling to group yoga sessions.

Who could have imagined all this just two decades ago? That is precisely the question this book answers. Such structural shifts in the nature of a city the size of Winston-Salem evolve over years and happen because of the imagination and tireless work of many people. "From Tobacco to Technology" captures their stories. I have had the privilege of knowing some of them.

When I arrived in Winston-Salem in 2012, Gayle Anderson was one of the first people with whom I had the pleasure of meeting. To know Gayle is to know the spirit of Winston-Salem. Both behind the scenes and in public, Gayle has been a champion for transitioning a city built on manufacturing and tobacco into a city that embraces technology and the arts and harvests it for future-proofing. She will, however, be the first to tell you she hasn't forged this path alone.

Doug Maynard's vision for leveraging existing strengths and assets of the city and using them to help Winston-Salem evolve into a hub for biomedical science and engineering has proven to be nothing short of prescient. From the formation of the Virginia Tech-Wake Forest School of Biomedical Engineering and Sciences, housed in part in Wake Forest Biotech Place, in 2003 to the recent announcement of undergraduate programs of Wake Forest University in biomedical sciences and engineering, Dr. Maynard has seen his vision come to fruition in ways and to lengths many could not even have imagined. But he persevered, and that vision has served as the fuel for the evolution of a new knowledge economy.

Richard Dean took that vision and greatly expanded it to new heights previously unimaginable. Today there are 145 developable acres dedicated to building this knowledge community, and Richard Dean spearheaded that vision. But that expansion wouldn't have been possible without the generous gift orchestrated by former R.J. Reynolds CEO Andrew Schindler – the donation to Wake Forest Baptist Medical Center of the shuttered factory buildings that now comprise some of the most modern and technologically advanced buildings ever built in our region. We also have my dear colleague Graydon Pleasants to thank for his tireless efforts acting as the catalyst to assemble the land mass and bring city officials, developers, architects, building planners, construction operations, and more together to make these buildings, these spaces, and this community a reality. Dan Cramer and his colleagues at Wexford Science + Technology have been our major real estate developer and have informed our emphasis on internal and external space activation of this place we call the Innovation Quarter. The unwavering support of Wake Forest Baptist Medical Center has been crucial throughout.

Tomorrow indeed belongs to those who hear it coming. It belongs to those bold enough to forge a path forward in the face of the changing landscape around them. Tomorrow belongs to communities willing and able to work together toward common goals. It belongs to leaders able to overcome roadblocks and who are undeterred by temporary setbacks.

One needs only to drive down Chestnut Street, walk through Bailey Park, or cross over Research Parkway to see what this place is now. This book tells the story of how it started.

While there is a clear vision for the future of Wake Forest Innovation Quarter, the future also has an interesting way of keeping us on our toes. I can't predict what the future holds, but I can promise this: the future of Winston-Salem – the City of Arts and Innovation, a community that has shown a tenacity in its ability to adapt to survive – will be anything but boring.

Eric Tomlinson
President, Wake Forest Innovation Quarter

PROLOGUE

R.J. Reynolds Tobacco Company held a groundbreaking ceremony for its new manufacturing plant in northwest Forsyth County on the morning of October 29, 1982. It was a suitably impressive occasion to mark the start of the single biggest investment Reynolds would ever make in tobacco manufacturing. More than 500 guests had been invited, including Governor Jim Hunt and his cabinet, members of the General Assembly, local elected leaders, representatives from agricultural and tobacco groups, and local business and education leaders.[1]

For the assembled dignitaries, the new factory was just the latest example of RJR's corporate might. Reynolds was the largest tobacco company in the world, and here, on 600 acres of farmland northwest of Winston-Salem, it was about to spend a billion dollars to build the largest cigarette plant in the world.[2]

Many in the public no doubt viewed the groundbreaking as the latest example of Reynolds' sheer dominance in the tobacco industry. But company officers viewed it differently. They knew that the plant they were about to build here outside Tobaccoville was essentially a defensive move. For years, RJR's market share had been steadily eroded by archrival Philip Morris and its ubiquitous Marlboro man. This new plant would be so efficient that it would enable the company to make more profit off every cigarette it sold. And for a company that sold more than 200 billion cigarettes a year, even a fraction of a penny of extra profit added up in a hurry.[3]

The festivities had started the evening before, when the company hosted a meet-and-greet over cocktails and dinner for representatives of the tobacco trade and southern agricultural media. On the site, hot air balloons shaped like packs of Winston and Camel cigarettes flew over the stage and a large tent had been set up to host the barbecue lunch to follow, with entertainment by a bluegrass band.[4]

But for the Reynolds executives organizing the ground-breaking, the primary goal for the day was to impart the sheer size of the plant, whose roof would enclose almost 2.5 million square feet – enough to cover 17 football fields. To dramatically illustrate this, RJR's public relations director originally envisioned a simultaneous release of large helium-filled balloons on 50-foot tethers that would outline the plant's exterior walls.[5]

When this proved to be too complicated, the idea was scaled back. The day before the groundbreaking, the PR staff came out and spent hours filling the balloons and carefully tying them to weights so they would bob four feet off the ground. When they were finished, the effect was every bit as overwhelming as they hoped it would be. This was going to be one BIG plant.[6]

When they arrived the next morning, however, the balloons lay listlessly on their sides – grounded by an unexpected cold snap that had contracted the helium. But the balloons were still along the perimeter. It might not look as festive, but the guests would still get the idea.[7]

In hindsight, some would come to see the failure of the balloons to take flight that morning as a metaphor for what lay in store for R.J. Reynolds. Before the decade was out, the high-flying company would be grounded, tag-teamed back to earth by Philip Morris' damn cowboy and a Yankee carpetbagger who would hijack their headquarters.

And yet, Tobaccoville also represented a future direction for Winston-Salem that no one in the audience – or on the dais, for that matter – could have imagined.

1 THE RISE AND FALL OF CAMEL CITY

Winston-Salem was a manufacturing town, and tobacco was its money machine. It had been that way ever since Richard Joshua Reynolds arrived in the town of Winston nine years after the Civil War to start a business making plug chewing tobacco.

Reynolds lived to see his company prosper beyond his wildest dreams, but he could never have imagined the way it would be making cigarettes at the massive Tobaccoville factory that RJR Tobacco opened in 1986 just northwest of the city.

Everything about the plant was on a scale that mocked conventional thinking. Every day, five days a week, it took more than 450 tons of tobacco and turned it into 500 million cigarettes. It performed this feat through an ingenious amalgamation of pipes, conduits, conveyor belts, automated machinery and self-guided mobile robots that absorbed bales of tobacco on one loading dock and discharged cases of cigarette cartons on another – with almost no human intervention.[1]

At Tobaccoville, computers ran the show, starting with bar codes applied to every bale of tobacco that entered the sprawling factory. From there each bale would be successively broken down, cleaned, cut, dried, flavored, and blended with other tobaccos before going through a gauntlet of automated machines that portioned out a precise amount of tobacco on to the rolling paper and then affixed the filter, assembled the cigarettes into packs, the packs into cartons, and the cartons into cases for shipment.[2]

No expense was spared in ensuring that Tobaccoville was absolutely the best of its kind in the world. The team of executives overseeing construction of the plant searched the world over for the best equipment they could find, making the plant an international wonder that used cigarette-making machines from Germany, packing machines from Italy and self-guided robots from the Netherlands.[3] To keep it all running smoothly, the plant had its own power plant, built at a cost of $50 million, that produced enough electricity to power more than 50,000 homes.[4]

The manufacturing prowess of the Tobaccoville plant gave solace to the citizens of Winston-Salem, whose civic pride had been wounded in 1983 when Reynolds surrendered to Philip Morris its crown as the world's largest tobacco company. RJR's fall was a tough blow for a community whose collective psyche was tied to the fortunes of this giant tobacco company. Virtually everyone in the city worked, or knew someone who worked, for Reynolds, and in their bones they knew that what was good for R.J. Reynolds was good for Winston-Salem.

It had been that way ever since 1913, when Reynolds introduced the Camel, a blended cigarette using Turkish tobacco. It was an instant sensation. A year after bringing out the Camel, Reynolds sold a half a billion of them – a measure of success that exceeded the company's wildest dreams. But that was just the beginning. By 1917 it was selling 12.5 billion Camels and by 1921, Reynolds was selling 18 billion, accounting for almost half of all cigarette sales in the United States. The impact on the bottom line was stunning. Company profits grew from $2.8 million in 1913 to $16.2 million in 1921, and by 1924 they would reach $23.8 million.[5] Inevitably, Winston-Salem acquired a new nickname: Camel City.

Reynolds' prosperity reverberated across the city as the businesses that served it enjoyed corresponding success, among them the Nissen Wagon Works Co., which became the nation's largest maker of wagons (used to haul tobacco to and within the factories), and Wachovia Bank and Trust, the repository of Reynolds' corporate accounts. Money that could be traced to Reynolds also played a role in starting other businesses that would become national brands, including Hanes Knitting Company, Hanes Hosiery, and Piedmont Airlines, which would grow to be the nation's eighth-largest carrier.

By 1924, the wealth and industry generated by tobacco made Winston-Salem and its surrounding area the undisputed economic engine of North Carolina, and one of the nation's leading manufacturing centers. It was home to the world's largest producer of tobacco products, the nation's largest manufacturer of men's knit underwear, and the South's largest manufacturers of woolen goods, wagons, inner tubes, and rubber tires. With all the raw materials imported to serve its factories, the city was the nation's seventh largest port of entry.[6] The population swelled as people flocked to the city to find jobs, making Winston-Salem the largest city in North Carolina during the 1920s.

The R.J. Reynolds Tobacco Building was the capstone of Winston-Salem's golden decade, and it immediately became the iconic symbol of Reynolds' wealth – and in no small measure, of Winston-Salem civic pride. The elegant 22-story skyscraper was the tallest building in North Carolina and boasted an ornate Art Deco lobby adorned with a gold-leaf ceiling, rare Benedict metal, and marble quarried in France, Belgium, Missouri and Vermont. When completed in 1929, it received such acclaim that its architects scaled it up and used it as the basis for their next commission, the Empire State Building.

Winston-Salem would lose its standing as North Carolina's largest city during the 1930s, surpassed by others that grew more aggressively. But the city remained a manufacturing powerhouse, and the moneyed families that ran the factories and mills shared their wealth with the community, endowing it with high schools, auditoriums, hospitals, stadiums, parks, and recreational facilities bearing their names. The companies they founded were equally generous in sharing their wealth with the community. More often than not, their executives chaired the charities and the capital campaigns to raise money needed to achieve the community's objectives, be it a new terminal at the airport, an arts council for the city, or assistance in relocating a college to the city.

World War II and the post-war boom that followed would further enlarge the city's employment base. Hanes Knitting, in particular, prospered with wartime contracts for its products.

The demands of wartime logistics enabled R.Y. Sharpe to start Pilot Freight Carriers in 1941, and persuaded Malcolm McLean to move his nascent trucking company to Winston-Salem in 1943. In 1946, Western Electric Company, attracted by the supply of skilled labor created by National Carbon Company's wartime plant in Winston-Salem to produce submarine batteries, opened the first of what would grow to five factories in Winston-Salem collectively known as its North Carolina Works. In 1962 the North Carolina Works would be placed under AT&T, Western Electric's parent company. Reynolds, too, was continuing its ascent, and in 1958 it would take its perch as the largest tobacco company in the world.[7] Times were good, and the city prospered.

But it would not last.

Reynolds was the first to feel the pinch. It had started with the dawning realization in the 1950s that smoking could cause lung cancer. Soon the company was fending off lawsuits brought by the families of deceased smokers, but the company routinely prevailed in court. The bigger concern for Reynolds was the steady march of Philip Morris' Marlboro brand, which became the nation's best selling brand in 1975. With the Marlboro man setting the pace, Philip Morris continued to steal market share from Reynolds throughout the 1970s. Reynolds fought back, and gained back market share a year here and a year there, but the trend was clear when RJR decided in the late 1970s that it needed to upgrade its manufacturing plants. In 1980, the company announced that it would spend billions of dollars to modernize its manufacturing facilities. The program included the new plant at Tobaccoville, an overhaul of its Whitaker Park plant, and a new 1.2 million square-foot factory downtown that would take the place of Factories 1, 12, 64, and 256.[8]

But other forces were stalking Reynolds. Throughout the 1960s and 1970s, the wrongful-death lawsuits kept coming, and the company was increasingly preoccupied with fending them off. Although Reynolds continued to prevail, smoking was losing its allure, putting more pressure on its market share even as the federal government began stepping up its regulation of tobacco. Production continued to drop. By the time Tobaccoville opened in 1986, further expansion was unwarranted. The plans for a new downtown factory were set aside.[9] Soon Reynolds would start reducing its work force as production from its downtown factories was gradually shifted to Tobaccoville.

Those employees fortunate enough to staff the new plant faced new challenges, however. Even as the plant was under construction, Reynolds realized that it needed a new kind of employee – a better-educated employee – to run the plant. This represented another sea change for the company. As long as anyone could remember, anyone with initiative, common sense, and a good work ethic could do well at Reynolds no matter what their formal schooling. Joe Inman, Reynolds' vice president of manufacturing and the executive who was in charge of the Tobaccoville plant, got his start sweeping floors and cleaning bathrooms soon after getting out of high school and worked his way up. His ascent took him higher into the company ranks than most, but his initial path was the norm: Start low, take whatever job you could to get a foot in the door, and move up. If you were a good worker, you were set for life. Reynolds paid better than any other company, had better benefits, and had a stock purchasing plan that gave the rank-and-file the pride of ownership in the company.[10]

For a workforce such as this, Tobaccoville and its computer-driven processes were a shock to the system. It was common for visitors to compare the plant's control rooms, packed with keyboards, control panels, and computer monitors, to something out of a science fiction movie. Knowing that the new plant would place new demands on its workers, the company contracted with Forsyth Technical Community College and paid employees to go to school while Tobaccoville was under construction. Some, it turned out, could not even read or write, a sobering fact the company learned when it began examining its canceled paychecks to see which employees were endorsing them with an "X."[11] Some employees resisted, but the company put together a committee of managers at all levels and sent them out to explain that with the new plant, "we're making the company better, we're making our products better, and we're making you better."[12] If the red-brick factories downtown, filled with machines operated by hand, embodied the past, the new plant at Tobaccoville with its high-tech systems represented the future, in more ways than one.

The Tobaccoville plant had not even been in operation for a year, however, when the community would suffer a far greater psychological blow than Reynolds' fall to number two in the pecking order of tobacco companies. And this blow was delivered from within, by F. Ross Johnson, the cookie executive who became part of Reynolds' leadership when the company bought Nabisco Products as part of its diversification to ensure continuing profitability in the face of declining cigarette sales.

Johnson was the polar opposite of the typical Reynolds executive, brash and flamboyant with a my-way-or-the-highway attitude that was the antithesis of Reynolds' avuncular corporate culture. Before arriving in Winston-Salem he had ruled Nabisco, headquartered in New Jersey, after engineering a coup d'etat that dethroned its previous CEO. When Reynolds Industries bought Nabisco it named Johnson second in the pecking order behind CEO Tylee Wilson in the new entity known as RJR Nabisco. Soon Johnson was at it again, wooing board members and plotting to replace Wilson. It didn't take long. In August 1987, the board – peeved after learning that Wilson had not told them about a new smokeless cigarette the company had been secretly developing – voted Wilson out and Johnson in as the new CEO of RJR Nabisco, effective Jan. 1, 1988. Fourteen days after taking the helm, Johnson achieved what he really wanted: At his suggestion, the board agreed to his plan to move the company headquarters to Atlanta.[13] The move was mostly symbolic – only about 300 jobs were leaving – but to a city and a populace whose identity was so closely linked to Reynolds, the announcement was devastating. However, by the time Johnson hijacked RJR Nabisco's headquarters, the city had suffered another loss, far more injurious in practical terms. On January 10, 1986, McLean Trucking, the nation's fifth-largest trucking company, filed for bankruptcy because of continuing losses following deregulation of the trucking industry.

McLean had been a small trucking company based in Fayetteville, NC, when Malcolm McLean moved the headquarters to Winston-Salem in 1943 to be closer to one of his prime customers, R.J. Reynolds.[14] By the time he sold the company in 1955 to develop a radical new concept in shipping using containers, McLean Trucking had 1,770 trucks and 32 terminals. It continued to grow under its new owners and had some 10,000 employees and more than 400 terminals, including almost 1,000 who worked out of its headquarters and terminal on Waughtown Street, when it declared bankruptcy.[15]

The city's leaders did not know, as they issued their carefully worded reactions to McLean's bankruptcy and the departure of Reynolds' headquarters, that Winston-Salem was in the early stages of a half-decade that would pummel the city's self-image and eviscerate its employment base.

The next blow came just seven weeks after the RJR move was announced: Piedmont Airlines, another homegrown success story headquartered in Winston-Salem, was bought by USAir. If Reynolds was the heart of Winston-Salem, Piedmont was its face to the world. Renowned for its hospitality and customer service, Piedmont served as Winston-Salem's – and by extension, North Carolina's – ambassador to the nation. The airline's new owners – who had been bitter rivals with Piedmont – quickly moved to remove any trace of the Piedmont brand and began shifting jobs to its other facilities. The buy-out eventually cost the city 5,100 jobs.[16]

Winston-Salem was on a losing streak, and the bad news kept coming. On January 25, 1988, AT&T announced that it would close its North Carolina Works on Lexington Road, throwing out of work 3,300 skilled employees who made suburban loop circuits and digital multiplexers for carrying multiple telephone signals over a single line. At the zenith of its presence in Winston-Salem, the company had employed 13,000, but that number had been gradually declining as advances in manufacturing allowed the company to maintain production with fewer employees – particularly after AT&T consolidated its various manufacturing facilities in 1974 in a massive facility on

Lexington Road that initially employed more than 6,000. In 1983, AT&T had reduced its workforce on Lexington Road by 3,000 employees, but this was not enough to save the rest. The company simply had too much production capacity for the demand, and in 1986 it decided to shift work from North Carolina to another plant in Oklahoma.[17]

Just ten months later, in October 1987, Ross Johnson struck again. This time he was bidding to take RJR Nabisco private in a leveraged buy-out – the "leverage" being the huge amount of debt the buyer would take on to make the purchase, and pay back by cutting costs and selling assets. But his plan went awry when others jumped into the bidding. The eventual winner was a New York investment firm virtually no one in Winston-Salem had heard of (save those who followed mergers and acquisitions) called Kohlberg Kravis Roberts & Co. Henry Kravis, the company's leader, moved RJR Nabisco headquarters to New York, cut 2,000 jobs, and placed the company in the hands of a former executive with American Express. Saddled with so much debt, the company was no longer in a position to provide more than token support for community endeavors.[18]

Reynolds Tobacco would continue to shed jobs. In July 1987 it announced that it would reduce its workforce by 2,300 by offering older employees early retirement. In March 1989, it laid off 700, and in August 1989, it cut another 1,640 positions.[19]

By then the city had lost another employer to bankruptcy – this time, Pilot Freight Carriers. Pilot had been founded in 1941 in Winston-Salem and was another source of civic pride, but the company was too small to compete in the dog-eat-dog world of deregulation. It was an ugly demise that played out in the local headlines over more than a year, but by April 1989, the company had laid off nearly all of its 2,650 employees, including the 700 who worked out of its local terminal and headquarters.[20]

By the time the 1980s came to a close, a city that had started the decade at the top of its game had been shaken to its core. To be sure, the city still boasted a robust number of manufacturing jobs, and civic boosters proclaimed the city's underlying strengths. But after five years of pummeling, city leaders had lost confidence in the future. What jobs remained, they had learned, could be lost at any moment, the latest victim of a buy-out, merger, or corporate streamlining. The closing of Reynolds' last downtown factory in June 1990 served as a symbolic coda to a five-year civic dirge. For 116 years, Reynolds had been manufacturing tobacco products downtown. That historic tie was now severed. Winston-Salem would have to find a new identity. The answer would come, improbably, from a radiologist at the Bowman Gray School of Medicine.

2 FALSE STARTS

The leveraged buy-out of RJR Nabisco brought the city another casualty, one unknown to all but a handful of people. It was a loss not of an asset, but of a plan – a plan that might have jump-started the city's transition to a new economy, brought new life to downtown, and spawned hundreds of new jobs.

The plan took seed within the headquarters of Reynolds Tobacco, where an old guard of executives were, in spite of their Yankee CEO, still trying to look out for the city. That the plan would also restore value to one of the company's biggest eroding assets – its obsolete downtown factories – made it all the better.

When Reynolds was on top of the tobacco world, before Ross Johnson and the merger of Reynolds and Nabisco, the company had settled on a long-term plan that called for razing its factories downtown after the Tobaccoville plant opened. In their place, Reynolds planned to build a modern cigarette factory with all the manufacturing efficiencies it had built into the Tobaccoville plant. However, by the time Tobaccoville opened, Reynolds' loss of market share and the falling demand for cigarettes eliminated the need for a new downtown factory. But that raised a new question for the company: what to do with its old factories, and the 110 acres of real estate they occupied downtown?

To assist the company, Hudnall Christopher, Reynolds' vice president for manufacturing, brought in a consultant. His recommendation: Use the land to create an employment base for the next generation by building a complex for high-tech manufacturing and applied research.[1]

On Hawthorne Hill two miles west of downtown, Dr. Richard Janeway, the dean of the Bowman Gray School of Medicine, caught wind of the plan and made plans to pay a visit to Reynolds with Dr. Douglas Maynard, the chairman of the Department of Radiology.

Maynard – aside from being one of Janeway's oldest friends – was the logical choice to go along, having spent the past three years lobbying for ways to enhance the medical school's technology research. Despite his family roots in rural North Carolina, Maynard grew up in Costa Rica, where he went at the age of 6 when his father moved there to open a Coca-Cola plant. He returned to the United States to attend Wake Forest College, majored in chemistry, found himself interested in medicine, and completed medical school at Bowman Gray intending to be a general practitioner. The draft was still in effect, so upon graduation Maynard entered the Army to fulfill his service commitment. While at Fort Lewis, the post commander assigned him to read X-rays in the afternoons, despite his lack of formal training in radiology. Maynard coped by reading every book he could find and consulting with a nearby radiologist when possible. The bug was planted. A year after his discharge, Maynard returned to Bowman Gray for a residency in radiology and became friends with Janeway, a fellow resident studying neurology.[2]

As a radiologist, Maynard depended as much as any doctor on the state of medical technology. His specialty grew out of the discovery of X-rays in 1895 and their wondrous ability to peer inside the body without cutting it open. Eight decades later, new technologies and the development of powerful computers had yielded magnetic resonance imaging and computed axial tomography, giving doctors new ways of seeing soft tissue. Slow though these early MRI and CAT systems were, they whetted radiologists' appetites for faster, better systems that might one day produce not just still images, but actual movies of a patient's tissue and organs.

Maynard could envision even more ways technology could revolutionize medicine. What if a patient's total medical record was available to any doctor? What if it could be implanted within the patient? What if doctors could "biopsy" diseased tissue from the outside? What if a patient's internal organs could be displayed in three-dimension holographs, or diseased tissue could be imaged and examined at the cellular level?[3] Making these dreams a reality required expertise that doctors did not possess, in physics, mathematics, and computer science, integrated by sound engineering. The problem, as Maynard saw it, was that Wake Forest did not have an engineering program that he could collaborate with.

But the issue was, literally, more than academic. Maynard had seen the trend. The medical schools that offered a significant research capability were attracting the best faculty and the best students. If Bowman Gray did not do something soon, it would descend into irrelevance. But he also knew that the school's leadership would do what it would take to prevent this – even, he feared, if that meant relocating to Charlotte or some other city that enabled it to "be a player."[4]

Maynard's agenda meshed nicely with Janeway's. Ever since becoming dean in 1971 he had the goal of making Bowman Gray part of the elite "NIH derby" – the top forty medical schools in the country in terms of research funded by the National Institutes of Health. At the time the school ranked in the mid-70s, and it was making little progress toward its goal. Anything that would bolster the school's research capability could only help.[5]

Bowman Gray Medical School's link to the statewide microwave network operated by the Microelectronics Center of North Carolina gave them a place to start. The network allowed institutions to exchange large amounts of data; Maynard envisioned using the system to send diagnostic images so doctors at one hospital could consult with experts at another. In June 1986, Maynard sent a memorandum to school administrators proposing that the medical school apply for a grant from the National Science Foundation to develop "a national resource" in medical communications engineering. The grant would allow Wake Forest to join forces with North Carolina State University, Duke University, the University of North Carolina at Chapel Hill, the Microelectronics Center, and industry partners to develop ways to send medical images by microwave.[6]

The university declined to apply for the grant, but by then, Maynard had moved on to the most important item on his agenda: getting Wake Forest to start an engineering program. Maynard had spent several months investigating the ways and means of accomplishing this, picking the brain of his friend Pete Santago, a graduate of Virginia Polytechnic Institute's engineering program. When the time was right, Maynard (with the blessing of Dick Janeway) broached the subject with John Anderson, Wake Forest's vice president for planning and administration, and prevailed upon Santago to set up a formal fact-finding trip to Virginia Tech.

On July 5, 1988, Maynard and Anderson made the two-hour drive to Blacksburg for a full day of meetings with school administrators. They had a long list of questions: What academic programs are the minimum necessary to have an engineering school? What physical facilities would it take? How much square footage do they require? How many classrooms, how many labs? How many faculty members does it require, and what is the going rate for engineering faculty salaries? What is the administrative overhead?[7]

Armed with this information, Maynard began sketching together a preliminary timetable. The first step: have Wake Forest President Thomas Hearn appoint a committee in the fall of 1988 to make a formal feasibility study. If all went according to the plan, the first students could be enrolled in the fall of 1991.[8]

Three weeks after Maynard's return from Blacksburg, he and Dick Janeway paid a call on Robert Emken, the executive vice president for administration at Reynolds Tobacco Co. Janeway, in his capacity as vice president for economic development for the Greater Winston-Salem Chamber of Commerce, had learned of Reynolds' plans to redevelop its downtown property. He immediately saw that Reynolds' plans might fit nicely with the medical school's interest in enhancing its technology capabilities.[9]

At the meeting, Emken briefed them on the plan and showed them a mock-up of what their downtown property might look like once it was redeveloped into a research park.[10]

Maynard could barely contain his enthusiasm. Here, in little scale models, was the means for achieving the vision he had been pursuing – a place where academic and industry researchers could collaborate in developing the next generation of medical technology while creating a new, high-tech employment base in the city. That afternoon, he dashed off a letter to Emken that fleshed out his thinking:

"What I see developing is an Applied Research Park with a theme that fits the industries in the community and educational programs in engineering and computer science at the undergraduate and graduate levels tailored to those areas. All educational institutions could be involved from the beginning, Winston-Salem State University, North Carolina State University, Wake Forest University including Bowman Gray School of Medicine.....

"The undergraduate programs could be located totally or in part at their respective institutions, however, it is conceivable that some of the specialty courses could be offered in the Research Park....

"With the appropriate theme for the park, which would certainly need to include industrial automation, communications and networking, it would be attractive for high technology companies to locate in the park and provide research programs and job opportunities for our students....

"Bob, what you and R.J. Reynolds Tobacco have started can quickly develop into a very significant educational and research program with an academic – industrial interphase that could be the 'shot in the arm' that Winston-Salem needs at this time."[11]

With no time to lose, Maynard told Emken he would contact John Anderson at Wake Forest, Chancellor Cleon Thompson at Winston-Salem State, and Chancellor Larry Monteith at NC State in hopes of pulling together a joint meeting with Emken the next week. He also said he would contact Harry Bosco, the president of the Medical Division of AT&T,

and ask him to meet with Emken, too.[12] AT&T had been the "industry partner" Maynard had in mind in the grant proposal he had submitted to the National Science Foundation; Reynolds' plans gave him a new way to lure them to Winston-Salem.

Maynard reiterated his thinking to John Anderson, the university's vice president for administration and planning, in a five-page letter on Aug. 3:

> "I believe that, if Reynolds carries through with their plan to establish an Applied Research Park in the downtown area, it would be a perfect time for us to start an Engineering School. The park would provide both research and job opportunities for our students.... With the facilities of the four universities, the use of the microwave network, the proper theme for the park, graduate engineering programs to 'fit' the interest of the industries involved, and the support of the community, the whole effort could be just what our community needs at this time to attract the proper type of industry to locate here. I have had recent conversations with the medical venture within AT&T with which we are working; they are interested in what is going to happen and might be talked into moving their company here."[13]

The fall of 1988 was filled with great expectations as the engineering initiative gained momentum. On November 10, Anderson sent a memorandum to Wake Forest President Tom Hearn, recommending that the school begin the process of starting an engineering program. "Only a resident engineering program which brings 'critical mass' of both faculty and students to Winston-Salem will serve the city's (and Triad's) long term needs....

"The concept is that of an engineering program, both undergraduate and graduate studies, located at Wake Forest University (on both campuses) plus an applied research facility at the downtown technology park.... We recommend that Wake Forest University sponsor a detailed study of an engineering school (undergraduate and graduate) in Winston-Salem and that R.J. Reynolds Tobacco Company furnish support for this study. They would be asked to participate in it. Reynolds would be <u>key</u> in the study of external clientele and their needs." (emphasis in the original)[14]

Meanwhile, Reynolds Tobacco included the topic of an applied research park in a survey it conducted of community perceptions about Reynolds and the future of the city. The final report on the survey reflected the medical school's concept of how the school and RJR might collaborate: "The key ingredient is the need for an engineering school in Winston-Salem. This could be at Wake Forest, Winston-Salem State, from North Carolina State University via microwave or a combination of the three."[15]

Before the leveraged buyout saddled R.J. Reynolds with debt, the company had been working on a plan to convert its downtown factories into an applied research park.
Photo by David Rolfe, courtesy of Winston-Salem Journal

But events rendered the survey obsolete by the time the results were compiled and sent to company executives in March 1989. The leveraged buy-out had saddled RJR Nabisco with enormous debt and its new owners were looking to cut costs. The plans for an applied research park, like the earlier plans for a new tobacco factory downtown, were quietly put on the shelf. Few people in Winston-Salem would ever know of what might have been.

Given the new climate at RJR Nabisco, Hearn told Anderson and Maynard to put any thought of an undergraduate engineering program on hold. Maynard, refusing to let the idea go, chose to focus on what Hearn had *not* said. "I would still like to move forward here at Bowman Gray with our graduate engineering effort," he wrote in a memorandum to Dick Janeway. "If we can develop a graduate engineering program here, perhaps Wake Forest can eventually start an undergraduate program at Wake."[16] Janeway agreed, and gave Maynard the green light to continue his pursuit.

He found a sympathetic ear with Jerry Long, who had retired in 1988 as the president of RJR Tobacco and was now serving as the vice chairman of the Forsyth County Commissioners. They met in mid-April, just as Pilot Freight's ugly demise was playing out in the pages of the Winston-Salem Journal. Long, like virtually every other community leader, was worried about the future of Winston-Salem. If an engineering program in Winston-Salem would make the city more attractive to potential employers, he was all for it. Maynard also spoke with Winston-Salem Mayor Wayne Corpening, a retired vice president with Wachovia Bank. Corpening and Long had both the political influence and the connections with the city's business establishment to facilitate Maynard's new idea: a consortium of community leaders and foundations that could fund the start of a graduate engineering program at Bowman Gray in conjunction with NC State.[17]

At the same time, he suggested, the consortium might also provide the $8 million to $10 million it would take to start the undergraduate engineering program at Wake Forest. Mindful of Hearn's directions, however, Maynard told Long they had to tread lightly on this subject: "Perhaps they (the consortium) could first agree to fund a feasibility study with the commitment of necessary funds to start an engineering school...if the results are positive. This would allow the ground work necessary to get the Reynolda campus faculty behind such an endeavor. Some people feel that the faculty in liberal arts would require a bit of politicking."[18]

Maynard was also working the foundations. Before his meeting with Long he sent the Whitaker Foundation an application, ultimately rejected, to "strengthen our joint research and educational program with NC State University."[19] He also met with Zachary Smith of the Z. Smith Reynolds Foundation to discuss possible funding of the undergraduate program.[20]

Maynard's trump card, however, was the seat he held on the board of the Chamber of Commerce, which gave him the opportunity to seek the support of the business community at large.[21] He stressed that the engineering program with NC State, and perhaps other schools, could serve not just Bowman Gray, but many other entities in town. For example, he said, the three-dimensional image processing technology needed for medical imaging could also be used to create special effects that could be taught at the film school that had recently been started by the NC School of the Arts. Information systems to track

Doug Maynard found a kindred spirit in Winston-Salem Chamber of Commerce executive Gayle Anderson.
Photo courtesy of Snyder Photography

patient scheduling and data could be used by Reynolds for inventory and production control, and digital data management for storing medical images could also be used by Wachovia Bank to store client records digitally.[22]

In a letter to Gayle Anderson, the chamber's executive vice president, Maynard imparted both his sense of urgency and the need for a patient, concerted effort: "My suggestion is one that has been put forward by a number of individuals and is certainly not the only solution. I do believe, however, that if the community got behind such a proposal, we could rapidly develop a plan and start moving forward. Although the community would like a 'quick fix' in regard to recruiting companies, a long-range plan is necessary when it comes to recruiting high-technology industries. The Research Triangle Park has been around for a long time. It is imperative, however, for us to get started."[23]

Although Fred Nordenholz, the chamber president, was more attuned to Winston-Salem's traditional reliance on manufacturing, Maynard found in Gayle Anderson a kindred spirit within the chamber. She was a former public relations executive with R.J. Reynolds who joined the chamber staff in 1989. She and Maynard were well acquainted with each other from shared community activities, and shortly after her arrival on the chamber staff Maynard lost no time in recruiting her to his cause. Over breakfast one morning, he shared his fears about the future viability of the medical school and presented his vision for an engineering program and technology park. Anderson did not need to be convinced; she was just as worried about Winston-Salem's future.[24] When Maynard presented his thoughts to the chamber board, she became his biggest advocate among the staff.

Having already secured the support of Long and Corpening and with Dick Janeway's membership on the chamber board supplying a ready second, Maynard soon had the board's endorsement of his plan to bring engineering to the city. He and Anderson now began working in earnest to build broader community support. By the end of 1989 a consensus had formed that the best approach was to develop a graduate engineering program related to the medical school and, out of that research, create a new avenue of economic growth for the city. The first step would be to get members of NC State's engineering faculty to set up shop in Winston-Salem. This strategy served two purposes: It would not only give the medical school the engineering presence it wanted, but, by involving a state-funded institution, it made it feasible to ask the N.C. General

Assembly to help bear the cost. However, to make such a request politically palatable and prevent inter-Triad rivalry from derailing the plan, the proposed engineering program would also involve Winston-Salem State and NC A&T universities too.[25]

To further sell the plan as a stimulus for economic development, the efforts of the various schools would be housed in an independent research institute. Mindful of Reynolds' defunct plan for an applied research park, Winston-Salem's leaders hoped that such an institute might yet be located somewhere downtown.[26]

With the community and school administration behind him, Maynard and a committee of like-minded colleagues set about preparing a formal proposal to present to the legislature.[27] Technically, the research institute would involve faculty from three institutions: Bowman Gray, NC State, and NC A&T. Winston-Salem State, lacking an appropriate graduate program, would not contribute faculty. But when it implemented its plan to offer graduate education in computer science, it would be invited to participate.

The initiative would be called the Piedmont Triad Graduate Engineering Program and initially would be housed on three floors of the MRI building on Hawthorne Hill. As the program grew it would move into a separate building. Finally, as a natural outgrowth of the research sponsored by the joint program, a research park would be created. "It is envisioned as a high technology park with tenants from the medical, software and light manufacturing industries; the park would encompass 100+ acres and would be zoned as mixed-use property with apartments, retail and offices."[28]

In the summer of 1990, with a draft proposal in hand, Maynard, Anderson, Nordenholz, and other supporters – notably Donald G. Haver – began making the rounds of the "stakeholders" in the plan. Haver was RJR's vice president for contributions and had been privy to RJR's proposal for an applied research park. Haver and Maynard were neighbors and during their chance meetings they had exchanged their concerns about the future of the city.[29] In the months and years to come, Haver would become an important ally behind the scenes in assisting the chamber's technology initiatives.

The chamber board enthusiastically supported the draft proposal, as did Mayor Martha Wood, who had recently succeeded Corpening as mayor. Wood and some board members, however, stressed the need to keep Winston-Salem State involved. In fact, WSSU Chancellor Cleon Thompson was more circumspect. Thompson knew that NC Central University had been left out when Research Triangle Park was formed in 1958 and that, despite the school's subsequent efforts, it had never been added as a participant. Mindful of that history, Thompson said he would support the plan under two conditions: that WSSU be included as a founding member of the consortium that owned that Piedmont Triad Research Institute (as the initiative was now being called), and that WSSU be an active participant in the program as it developed its graduate program in computer science. The institute, Thompson believed, might help his school establish the graduate program sooner rather than later.[30]

Pete Santago and Maynard next went to Greensboro to present the plan to Chancellor Edward Fort of NC A&T and other senior administrators. Heretofore, discussions with A&T had been conducted informally between Santago and Harold Martin, the dean of A&T's engineering school. They were old friends, having attended graduate school together at Virginia Tech, where their offices were across the hall from each other.[31]

In a meeting that lasted nearly two hours, Maynard and Santago spelled out their plan and how A&T fit into the picture, and were rewarded with A&T's enthusiastic support. Fort had long been seeking to add several doctoral programs; the Piedmont Triad Graduate Research Institute might well be the vehicle to make it happen. The institute also held the promise of helping A&T reach its goal of securing $40 million in funded research programs by 2000, an almost three-fold increase from its current base. In a memorandum to Hearn, Maynard reported, "His enthusiasm for the project appears genuine, and he strikes me as a very energetic, dynamic individual who has the future and A&T clearly tied to 'Triadism.' He should be an asset in gaining legislative support from the Guilford delegation."[32]

Although support from the Guilford delegation would be crucial once the proposal was before the General Assembly, the plan would go nowhere if Forsyth County's legislators would not introduce it. To secure their support, Nordenholz, Anderson, and Maynard held a series of meetings and phone conversations one-on-one with Representatives Lyons Gray, Annie Brown Kennedy, Frank Rhodes, and Theresa Esposito, and Senators Marvin Ward and Ted Kaplan after the elections in November 1990. All saw the merits of the plan, but they also knew the state was facing a tight budget year. Ward suggested that, rather than include the money in the appropriation for the University of North Carolina system, the best approach might be to create a separate bill to fund the start-up program. However, he counseled that the city take no further action until the General Assembly met in January, at which time committees would be appointed and a strategy could be plotted.[33]

The engineering institute had no chance of winning legislative approval without the backing of all hands at Wake Forest, so on Dec. 11, 1990, at Hearn's request, Maynard presented the proposal to the Reynolda cabinet of university vice presidents. Afterwards, in a frank memo to Maynard, provost David G. Brown warned that success might not come immediately. "Persevere. Big ideas like yours are rarely funded when they are first proposed to the legislature.... I suggest you structure the venture in a way that will allow you to be successful this year, and also to build on the work of this year during the next legislative session if that is necessary." And, he said, Maynard must keep "any conversation regarding undergraduate engineering education very much in the background.... We can expect all existing engineering schools to resist the movement."[34]

Over the holidays and into the new year, Maynard et al. continued to build support for their strategy. On Jan. 31, 1991, a working group drawn from the four schools convened to discuss the nuts and bolts of how the institute would be organized and funded. The other schools endorsed the proposed legislative approach and agreed to develop a strategy to raise $2.5 million from the community to help cover operating costs for the first five years. Haver agreed to chair a committee, formed under the Chamber of Commerce, to raise the money.[35]

With all four schools on board, the committee began working to gain broader legislative support. With the help of Rep. Lyons Gray (the grandson of the man who gave his name to the medical school), a joint meeting was held in Raleigh with the members of the Forsyth, Guilford, and Wake County delegations, where the proposal was pitched as an economic development project.[36] A separate meeting was held with Rep. David Diamont of nearby Surry County, who chaired the House Appropriations Committee. With the endorsement of all concerned, Gray agreed to draft and introduce a bill, which would be jointly sponsored by all three delegations, to establish the research institute. State funding, however, was very much in doubt. The national economy was in recession and state revenues were coming up short. Mindful of this, the request for funding would be made in a separate bill. (This would be further refined into two bills, one for start-up money and another to cover operating costs.)

The bill authorizing the institute was introduced on April 18.[37] Among other things, the bill called for the institute to be phased in for the 1991-1992 academic year and instructed the UNC Board of Governors to adopt rules to implement the provisions of the legislation.[38] Gray began circulating it to gain support, and was rewarded for his efforts with the unsolicited endorsement of House Speaker Dan Blue.[39]

In due course the House Education Committee approved the bill and forwarded it to the floor of the House, where it was approved, sent to the Senate, and approved again. On June 18, the General Assembly ratified the bill into law.

For Doug Maynard, Gayle Anderson, Don Haver, Pete Santago and the many others who had devoted the past several years to the fight to bring engineering to the Triad, it was a deeply satisfying moment. More challenges lay ahead, as they had yet to secure a base for recurring funding of the institute. But nothing could have happened until they had the state's blessing. And that battle had been won. Or so they thought.

3   OPERATION PINETREE

The band of visionaries promoting Winston-Salem's would-be high-tech economy must have thought all the planets were aligning in their favor. Just as the legislature was approving the start-up money for the Piedmont Triad Graduate Research Institute, a prime location came on the market for the research park they wanted to develop for the new ventures that all this research would spin out.

It was in southeastern Forsyth County, roughly in the center of the triangle formed by Winston-Salem, Greensboro, and High Point, with a mile of frontage on the new stretch of Interstate 40. Pinetree Golf Course comprised the largest parcel, but combined with other tracts of farmland on the periphery, the site totaled 1,000 acres.[1]

The site seemingly had every trait anyone could want for a Triad research park. It was big enough, but not too big. It was in a neutral location and convenient to all three cities. Its frontage on I-40 gave it both easy access and visibility. And it was suitably pastoral for the campus-like setting that was expected for research parks.

The rural site was the polar opposite of the downtown factory district where Reynolds had proposed to develop an applied research park. Doug Maynard had seized on Reynolds' proposal because at the time it was the best chance he saw for bringing high-tech research and engineering to the city. But a clone of Research Triangle Park was what Maynard really had in mind: an expansive, landscaped campus dotted with clean, high-tech companies pursuing their dreams of a better tomorrow without the noise, bustle, and congestion of the city. Early on – before the RJR factories entered the conversation –

Maynard and Gayle Anderson had paid a call on Archie Davis, the man who made the real RTP a reality, to get advice on how to develop such a park here.

In 1958, Gov. Luther Hodges recruited Davis to resuscitate the flagging effort to establish a research park that Hodges had proposed as a way to diversify North Carolina's economy and provide opportunities for the graduates of the state's universities. The park originally was established as a for-profit development, but the private sector had not stepped up to provide the capital to assemble the land. Davis, the chairman of Wachovia Bank & Trust, agreed to help – on the condition that the park be turned into a non-profit entity – and then raised the necessary money within a month. Davis was long retired from Wachovia when he invited Maynard and Anderson to take a seat in his living room to discuss what it would take to develop a research park here. Like David Brown, the Wake Forest provost, Davis counseled perseverance. Even though RTP opened for business in 1959, it took years to attract the caliber of employers that were envisioned when it was proposed.[2]

Maynard had quickly pivoted to the idea of a downtown research park when the Reynolds factories came into the picture, but just as quickly switched back to Plan A when the leveraged buyout mooted that possibility.[3] In their hearts, Maynard, Anderson and the others behind the city's technology initiative were much more interested in creating a "real" research park for the Triad. This is what the market expected. And now, for $14 million, the Piedmont Triad could get into the game.

As fortuitous as the timing might have been, it was almost too much of a good thing. The chamber's Technology Committee, established to oversee the development of a technology economy, was still trying to raise $2.5 million to cover the operating costs of the graduate research institute for the next five years, and now it was faced with raising $14 million more to secure this land before it was carved up into subdivisions and shopping strips. But the timing could not be helped. Opportunities such as this rarely present themselves, and fortune favors the bold. So the Technology Committee mobilized for action to implement "Operation Pinetree."

In a presentation prepared for potential contributors, the committee described Operation Pinetree as "a two-pronged strategy to bring engineering and computer science education and research to the Piedmont Triad, along with high technology business and industry" – the two prongs being the graduate research institute and what they called the "Piedmont Triad Technology Campus."[4]

The research institute would serve not only as an incubator for new high-technology businesses, but also as a resource for continuing education in engineering and computer science for the employers already in the area. With pledges totaling $1.5 million in hand, the committee still needed $1 million to finance the first five years of the institute's operations. By then, the institute would be generating enough money through research grants and contracts to support itself. To complement this, the General Assembly would be asked for $750,000 a year to cover the cost of the faculty and students from public universities who would study at the institute.[5]

As for the technology campus, the committee members admitted this was a "visionary step." But, they argued, it would accelerate the economic growth that the research institute would foster by providing a suitable location for high-tech employers. And it would tangibly embody the long-espoused – but never quite realized – concept of "Triadism." The technology campus could serve not only initiatives spun out of the research institute, but perhaps the joint research center in engineering and science long sought by NC A&T and the University of North Carolina at Greensboro, and even the nascent Nutrition Research Center at Bowman Gray, which Congress had recently authorized to study ways that diet and nutrition could reduce the incidence of chronic diseases.[6] "We felt we needed to include High Point and Greensboro," Gayle Anderson said. "We thought it was bigger than Winston-Salem and when we did our projections we wanted to take full advantage of everything we had in the region."

The technology committee's pitch ended with a three-fold call to action: to begin negotiations immediately for the proposed campus; to gain the necessary endorsements by private and public organizations; and to identify sources for the money to buy the land.[7] The chamber board agreed, but with one caveat: The committee's pitch for buying the tract was predicated on its assumption that the research park would be populated by high-tech start-ups that would be spun out of the research at the institute, and by other high-tech companies. But that was an assumption that had never been tested. Before the chamber could, in good faith, ask the community – and the other communities in the Triad – to put up $14 million to buy a research park, it needed to have some independent verification that such a park made sense.

The first order of business was to raise $500,000 to buy out the option on the land, which had been taken by a developer in Guilford County. This would keep the tract intact while the chamber conducted a feasibility study on the proposed park – which would require $60,000 to $80,000 more that they hoped to raise from local foundations. Assuming the feasibility study validated the idea, the option would then buy time to raise money to buy the land.[8]

As for the feasibility study, Anderson had a good idea of who could do it. She had recently attended a conference in Salt Lake City sponsored by the American Association of University Research Parks, and had been impressed with the presentation by Vernon George, the managing partner of Hammer, Siler, George Associates, an economic and development consulting firm based in McLean, Virginia, just outside Washington, D.C. Anderson sought out George after his presentation and learned that he knew

Vernon George thought the idea of building a suburban park was probably off-base.

Photo courtesy of Vernon George

the Carolinas well, being a graduate of the University of North Carolina and having studied the Research Triangle Park and many other research parks across the United States. The more she talked with him, the more he struck her as a good choice to determine if their assumptions were on target.[9]

But in short order the game plan went awry. Local foundations were not in a position to grant that kind of money without a formal grant proposal and review. Had the committee found the $500,000 to option the land, it might have been able to wait on the grant cycle. As it was, the money was not forthcoming, giving committee members a palpable sense of urgency. It would simply take too long to write grant proposals and submit them with the next round of funding requests. Nor was there any certainty of being funded. In preliminary conversations with foundation directors, the chamber learned that they were not keen on funding economic development projects.[10]

The chamber board, not willing to let this opportunity slip away, decided to put up the money itself. In short order it issued an RFP and by the end of the year, Hammer, Siler, George Associates was under contract. Its work would be overseen by the chamber's Technology Committee.

Five months later, Vernon George would tell them that their thought of creating a research park was on target – but probably off-base.

Before validating the merits of the Pinetree location, HSG first had to determine if a Triad research park could attract enough tenants to justify its existence. There was a lot of competition. Starting with the first two research parks in the country established in the 1950s, Stanford Research Park in Palo Alto, California, and Research Triangle Park, there were now more than 125 research parks across the country affiliated with universities, and many other private-standing parks.[11] Clearly, Winston-Salem wasn't the only community trying to transform its economy by turning to technology.

Nonetheless, the Triad had a few things working in its favor, starting with the growing sophistication of local manufacturers as evidenced by the automated wonder that was the Tobaccoville plant. Likewise, the Westinghouse plant north of Winston-Salem produced turbine blades using very sophisticated machinery. So did the Deere-Hitachi plant in Kernersville, which, like Tobaccoville, relied on robotics and automated machinery.

The area also was a growing center for computing and information technology. Wachovia Bank, American Express, Sara Lee, USAir, and AT&T all operated major computerized facilities in the Triad, for data management or customer service.[12]

At Bowman Gray Medical School, the Radiology Department that Maynard chaired was at the forefront in exploring new ways of using digital technology to capture, store and transmit images. The technology promised to have wide-ranging applications to many other industries. Also at the medical school, the new Center for Research on Human Nutrition and Chronic Disease Prevention, recently authorized by Congress and for which the school had just broken ground, presented perhaps the most promising opportunity. Although it would take three years or more to complete the building, the center eventually was to employ 350 scientists, some of whom would be assigned to work closely with private industry. Already, Campbell's soups, Kellogg's cereals, and M&M Mars had approached Bowman Gray about collaborating with the center.[13,14]

Elsewhere in the Triad, NC A&T had an engineering school that was in the process of adding doctorate programs in mechanical and electrical engineering. Its Center for Composite Materials Research received money from NASA and the Defense Department. NASA had also just authorized creation of a Center for Aerospace Research at the school, and NC A&T was a member of the agency's Mars Mission Research Center. Like Bowman Gray, NC A&T was linked by the state microelectronics network to NC State.[15]

Finally, the new film school that the North Carolina legislature had authorized at the NC School of the Arts offered yet-unknown possibilities, given that industry's reliance on using the latest technology in imaging techniques. Maynard, for one, had already realized the overlap between what he wanted to do with digital radiology and the potential it offered the film industry, and was discussing possible joint programs with Sam Grogg, the dean of the new film school.[16]

But in many other respects, the Triad faced an uphill climb.

Despite the presence of Wake Forest, NC A&T, Winston-Salem State, the NC School of the Arts, Forsyth Technical Community College, and its counterparts in other Triad counties, overall, "from the standpoint of resources for research and technology development, the current mix of educational programs lacks the depth of nationally recognized research generally associated with the country's more successful research parks," HSG noted. Yes, the medical school presented opportunities, but it did not offer "the range and depth of engineering and science programs and courses typically required to support technology-based industry."[17]

Likewise, the area was poorly positioned to supply the labor force to support a research park. As a manufacturing center, Winston-Salem had thrived by offering an abundant pool of workers with a good work ethic and the willingness to learn the skills to operate sophisticated machinery. However, managers of the area's existing technology-based companies told the consultants that they had a hard time finding local engineers with the technical expertise they needed. "Most are forced to recruit from outside of the area." While the Triad's high quality of life helped, "lack of programs for continuing education in engineering at the graduate level has been a serious negative factor for some engineers who have rejected offers from Triad-based companies."[18] The Piedmont Triad Graduate Research Institute held the promise of remedying this shortcoming, but it was still in its infancy.

Finally, the high-tech start-ups that the research park was hoping would fill the park would require seed money in the form of venture capital, and here too, HSG reported, the supply was limited. "The Piedmont Triad has no base of active venture capitalists nor a network of individual investors who are familiar with technology-based industries and interested in investing in start-up companies. While that by itself is not a fatal flaw, it will constrain the number and potential success of new local companies which might find a research and technology park location desirable."[19]

To improve the odds of success, HSG chose to be liberal in looking at potential tenants, to include not only facilities for basic or applied research, but facilities for manufacturing and assembly by technology-based companies. However, for these needs, there were already plenty of existing business parks in the Triad that offered the amenities, controlled development, and heavy landscaping typical of a research park.[20]

(RTP) Research Triangle Park, the prototype that park advocates envisioned when they proposed building a research park on Pinetree Golf Course and the surrounding land.
Photo courtesy of Research Triangle Park

To gain a better picture of how a Triad research park would fare, HSG looked at ten other research parks across the nation that it deemed comparable to the proposed park in the Triad, based on the characteristics of the community, their location, and their associated educational institutions.[21]

They ranged from Research Triangle Park, the largest at 6,500 acres and the acknowledged gold standard of research parks, to the Northwestern University/Evanston Research Park with 24 acres. The Hopkins Bayview Research Campus, affiliated with Johns Hopkins University, deviated from the norm in that it did not offer the typical campus-like setting. It was an urban campus dominated by institutional development related to the university and its affiliated medical center.

In many respects, the most successful was the University of Utah Research Park in Salt Lake City. Founded in 1970 on 320 acres, the park had 25 buildings with a total of 1.8 million square feet of office and laboratory space. Of this, offices and laboratories affiliated with the university occupied only 150,000 square feet of space. An average of 86,500 square feet of new space was being leased every year by non-university users, and the park had 45 companies with a total of 4,500 employees.[22]

Closer to home, a Triad park would compete not only with Research Triangle Park, but three others in the Carolinas: the University Research Park north of Charlotte, affiliated with UNC-Charlotte; the Carolina Research Park, affiliated with the University of South Carolina in Columbia; and Clemson Research Park, affiliated with Clemson University.

Like the University of Utah Research Park, the Massachusetts Biotechnology Research Park illustrated the dramatic success possible when sufficient market demand existed: Established in 1985 on 75 acres in Worcester, Mass, only 15 acres were still available. The first building was completed in 1987; now there were four, occupied by 18 tenants with 550 employees, not counting a huge, 485,000-square-foot facility under construction for BASF Corporation. One reason for the park's success: "Its presence in the Boston region, with its extensive base of biotechnology companies and the educational resources available from M.I.T. and other universities."[23]

Conversely, the Clemson Research Park proved the risk of building a research park without sufficient demand. Since its founding in 1983, the park had attracted just three tenants to its 266 acres, including a Clemson University computer systems facility with 90 employees and the Clemson University environmental science engineering program with 40 faculty

and 100 students. The only private-sector tenant was
ChemWaste Management Services, with 60 employees.[24]

Clearly, as evidenced by Clemson's dim success, market
demand would be key to the fate of a Triad research park. HSG
gauged demand by looking at two key factors: The number and
size of businesses that might be attracted to the park; and university initiatives and relationships. "The relationship between
the strength of the university research efforts and research park
demand can be instructive," HSG noted. "The amount of sponsored research is a good indicator of how highly governmental
and private industry scientists rate an institution's research
effort."[25]

Toward that end, HSG compared the amount of sponsored
research with the lease rates in research parks. Clemson, with
$34 million in research awards, was leasing just 110 square feet
annually for every million dollars of research. The University of
Utah, with $110 million in research grants, was leasing 704
square feet. An anomaly was the Massachusetts Biotechnology
Research Park: With just $50 million in sponsored research, the
park was leasing 1,136 square feet annually for every million in
research. This, HSG noted, reflected the advantage of locating
in a region with a high concentration of high-tech and bio-tech
companies. "The shared pool of experienced labor, networking
and joint ventures are important advantages. Employees of
existing technology-based firms often leave to form their own
companies, thus accelerating the pace of new company forma-
tions and building space absorption."[26]

HSG adjusted the raw numbers to reflect the disparity in the
base of high-tech companies within each research park's metropolitan area. It further adjusted the numbers to account for the
availability of venture capital to support high-tech start-ups.
The adjustments reflected Utah's success: It was leasing 535
square feet annually for every million dollars in sponsored
research. The park in Massachusetts, once adjusted, came in
second at 273 square feet.[27]

Applying these formulas to the Triad, HSG noted that with
a total of $64 million in sponsored research between Bowman
Gray, Wake Forest, NC A&T and UNC-Greensboro, a Triad park

could lease 7,040 square feet of space per year if it did no better than Clemson. If it were as successful as the park in Utah, it would lease 34,240 square feet a year. Based on the Triad's relative strengths, the company projected that actual absorption would range from 15,000 to 30,000 square feet per year.[28]

These numbers did not include the Triad's proven success in attracting information processing centers and technology-intensive manufacturers. Accounting for these uses, potential demand almost tripled. But, HSG noted, a Triad research park should not count on them. "The region's ability to attract and accommodate such facilities is not dependent on a research park. Historically, such facilities have been accommodated in traditional business parks and on campus sites throughout the region."[29]

What lessons did the study hold for the Triad? A number of factors – location, amenities, and neighborhood environment – influence the ability of research parks to attract tenants, HSG said. "The greatest variation, however, may result from the differences in project execution.... Effective marketing is a key to a research park's ultimate success. An important component of that marketing effort must be the park's relationship to the university, both in terms of identifying and persuading potential tenants and in making available university resources to the park tenants."[30]

Overall, the report supported the concept of building a research park in the Triad. But it came with one caveat familiar to every business leader in the community:

> "Collectively, the Triad has good potential for technology development. Individually, the three primary counties are much more limited in what they can offer technology-based companies. There is little history of cooperative efforts in the Triad. Parochialism and jealousies among the Triad cities and counties have keep the region effectively split into at least three separate entities. 'Triadism' has been a major goal for industrialists, business leaders and other forward-thinking community leaders. Research and technology development in the region

cannot work any other way. It is only through cooperative regional efforts that the Triad will be able to
compete for new technology-based industry."[31]

Even with this cautionary note, the members of the chamber's Technology Committee were heartened by the overall positive tone in the report. But inter-Triad jealousies were not the
only obstacles they faced. While HSG was compiling its report,
the committee had been preoccupied with fending off a new
threat – one that almost put a stop to the whole engineering
initiative before it ever got started.

4 Engineering the Triad

The rosy feelings in Winston-Salem when the General Assembly authorized the Piedmont Triad Graduate Research Institute were not shared in Chapel Hill, where the board of governors for the University of North Carolina took umbrage at what they considered ill-advised political meddling in their affairs.

They were particularly offended by language dictating that the board "shall adopt rules, after consultation with the board of directors of the Piedmont Triad Research Institute, to implement this article as it affects the University of North Carolina's and the designated constituent institutions' ongoing roles in the Piedmont Triad Graduate Engineering Program and in the education and research projects of the Institute."

The legislation was all the more galling because it was telling them how to fix a problem – the lack of graduate engineering programs in the Piedmont Triad – that they had already identified and were working to rectify.

In early 1990 the board of governors had initiated a review of the institutional missions of all 16 campuses in the UNC system.[1] Based on the results of this review, the board had come to the conclusion that the Triad area needed a greater engineering "presence" to support economic development. Toward that end, its 1991-1993 budget request to the General Assembly included money to establish a "Northern Piedmont Engineering Research Center,"[2] only to see that request ignored while the Forsyth County delegation finessed the legislature into approving the Piedmont Triad Graduate Research Institute. As envisioned by the governors, the center would be administered by NC State, housed at Winston-Salem State, and include

NC A&T.[3]

Although the Piedmont Triad Graduate Research Institute authorized by the legislature was similar in concept, there were two important distinctions in the eyes of the board members: It included a private institution – Wake Forest University – that was not accountable to the UNC board, and it set up a separate board of directors for the institute.

At a meeting of the board of governors in October 1991, C.D. Spangler Jr., the president of the UNC system, voiced doubt about the arrangement: "It appears to require that our engineering schools be responsible for the operation of research and education programs that are under the authority of the director and board of a separately chartered institute."[4]

Wilbur Meyer, the dean of the NC State University College of Engineering, agreed. "If the system institutions are going to be involved in engineering research activities that are state-supported in the Triad area, then the state institutions should be the chartered entity.... I think the issue is whether the state, which already has charted institutions, should abandon those and go to some other model."[5]

Reduced to its simplest terms, the board was declaring a turf war over who would control the program.

Rep. Lyons Gray, who had led the legislative effort, thought that it was a little late for UNC administrators to balk. Representatives of NC State had been party to the discussions that led to the new institute. Furthermore, faculty and students at NC State were already collaborating with their counterparts at Bowman Gray School of Medicine on research involving magnetic resonance imaging via the microwave network operated by the Microelectronics Center of North Carolina. "It sounds like they're trying to sandbag an already existing program," he told a reporter for the Raleigh News & Observer.[6]

But the UNC administration was not the only entity expressing qualms about the new institute. The chancellors of UNC-Greensboro and NC A&T were sounding less than enthusiastic about the graduate research institute.

Ten months earlier, in January 1991, the two universities had jointly announced plans to establish a $20 million

Engineering and Science Research Center, to be developed over the next 13 years, to serve its graduate students and local businesses.[7] The proposed center grew out of the 1990 institutional review the board of governors had ordered, and in many ways mirrored the governor's own proposed Northern Piedmont Engineering Research Center.[8]

As had the UNC board, the backers of the Greensboro-based initiative had watched the legislature authorize what they viewed as "Winston-Salem's" engineering initiative while theirs was ignored, and they were not any happier about it than their counterparts in Chapel Hill. "We believe the Engineering and Science Research Center represents the Triad's best hope for accelerating advanced engineering and science research here," said Chancellors Edward Fort of NC A&T and William Moran of UNC-G in a joint statement. Toward that end, they welcomed the UNC Board of Governors' scrutiny. "We believe it will, among other things, yield a clear and more general understanding of the ESRC proposed by NC A&T and UNC-G."[9]

The leaders of the Winston-Salem institute were taken aback by the sudden controversy. NC A&T had been an enthusiastic supporter of the bill to create the Piedmont Triad Graduate Research Institute. Moreover, the institute in Winston-Salem would concentrate on medical-related engineering, leaving other engineering research to NC A&T and UNC-G.[10] For that reason, their vision of the proposed Triad research park on the Pinetree Golf Course site included both institutions.

And as for the board of governors' concerns about governance, Gray had based the charter for the Piedmont Triad Graduate Research Institute on the charter for the Research Triangle Institute, which involved both public (UNC) and private (Duke) universities.[11]

However, since no provision had been made for UNC-G in the Piedmont Triad Graduate Research Institute, and since only the institute, and not the Engineering and Science Research Center, had been authorized by the General Assembly, Fort felt compelled to support UNC-G in its objections. Much as Vernon George was discovering that fall, "Triadism" only went so far. The fact was that the Piedmont Triad Graduate Research

Institute initially was to be housed in Winston-Salem. And even if it moved out to a neutral site at Pinetree between the three cities of the Triad, it was still going to be in Forsyth County, with all the attendant growth benefiting Forsyth's tax base.

Furthermore, with the institute already established by the legislature, it would have a head start in securing state funding, putting the Engineering and Science Research Center at a further disadvantage.

Given all these concerns, the UNC Board of Governors' objections gave Fort and Moran a new opportunity to fight for their own slice of the pie.

Spangler made it clear that his concern chiefly was one of resources. "From the standpoint of the university, more research is beneficial.... We recognize that our schools of engineering and our advanced scientific research programs are resources that are of benefit to the entire state, and we want these resources to be helpful in fostering economic development."[12] However, declarations that the two engineering programs would complement each other notwithstanding, the board feared that they "could place the engineering schools and NC A&T and NCSU in conflicting situations and could lead to a dissipation of their resources and energies by putting into place a series of expensive and uncoordinated activities."[13]

Given the legislative mandate to establish the Piedmont Triad Graduate Research Institute, the board was not in a position to ignore the Winston-Salem initiative in favor of its own proposal. So it did the next best thing: It appointed six of its members to form a committee to study the issue, under the leadership of Phil Carson of Asheville. Winston-Salem officials were happy to see that the committee included two members – Martha McNair and Benjamin Ruffin – from Winston-Salem.[14]

Nonetheless, the committee did not get off to a promising start. At its first meeting, in November 1991, the founding president of the Research Triangle Institute slammed the planning for the Piedmont Triad Graduate Research Institute for being "naïve" and "hastily drawn." George Herbert said that the institute in the Triad may have been modeled after the Research Triangle Institute, but there was a critical difference between the two: unlike the Triad institute, the Research Triangle Institute was not created or financed by the state. "These institutes have to run like businesses," he said. "They have to be entrepreneurial, hungry and lean and not look to some permanent, sustaining source of money."[15]

Lynn Preston, the deputy director of the engineering centers division of the National Science Foundation, was equally dubious. Successful engineering research centers require a tremendous amount of coordination and pursue research in several areas. Winston-Salem's vision of a Triad institute focused on medical-related research would not only be too narrowly drawn, but it would rely on a research sector that was fraught with potential pitfalls. "I wouldn't start with the medical industry," she told the committee. "That's tough. They are very close with their contracts and do not want to collaborate."[16]

Gayle Anderson did her best to explain the precedent for governance of the institute, and that the state was only paying for salaries of state university faculty – not the institute's administrative costs. But some committee members seemed more interested in pursuing a different route.[17]

A month later, the committee held a meeting in Winston-Salem to hear from community leaders, not just from Winston-Salem but also Greensboro and other cities in the Triad. At that meeting, the Triad representatives pulled out all the stops in making the case that the region needed both the Piedmont Triad Graduate Research Institute and the Engineering and Science Research Center. The roster of speakers included Fort and Moran, representing their two universities; Dick Janeway, representing Bowman Gray, U.S. Rep. Steve Neal, whose Fifth Congressional District included Winston-Salem; Alex Spears, the vice chairman of Lorillard Corp. in Greensboro; Jim Johnson, the new president of RJR Tobacco; John Medlin, the CEO of First Wachovia Corp.; Jim Melvin, the president of First Home Federal Savings and Loan in Greensboro (and the president of the committee proposing the Engineering and Science Research Center); William Klopman, the retired chairman of Burlington Industries; David Phillips, the president of Phillips Industries in High Point; and Kenneth Rashke, the retired manager of AT&T's North Carolina Works.[18]

The group made a well-orchestrated case, Maynard said. "Gayle and I lined up every major CEO in this city, every major player, and she gave them all a script and I mean to tell you, you would have thought this program was the best thing in the world."[19]

Their core message was that the Triad was already reaping some benefit from the early steps to give the Triad an engineering presence, and that the committee should allow the community to stay the course. "It is not just a dream," Medlin said, "but a reality that is, even if in a small sense, working." Johnson echoed that thought: "It is an important place to begin because...it has already attracted industry," alluding to a team of engineers that Bell Labs had working at the Medical School to work on filmless radiology storage and transmission. That technology could then be applied to banking, data processing, and reservation systems. Maynard noted that the institute, by itself, would not carry the Triad's economy. "This is a niche. But you have to start somewhere, and you might as well start with what is working."

And to underscore that the *raison d'etre* for this initiative was to stem the area's loss of jobs, Raschke noted that the huge AT&T Works plant in Winston-Salem might well have kept its operations in Winston-Salem if its employees had access to engineering education. "If North Carolina State was here, it is my judgement AT&T would now have a payroll here of $350 million," he said.[20]

After the lobbying onslaught, Carson, the committee chairman, joked, "I've heard of dog-and-pony shows, but this was a herd of elephants!"[21]

Afterward, the committee toured the radiology labs and explored their options with representatives of the medical school. When the committee broached the idea of somehow combining the three engineering proposals, Maynard and Janeway expressed tentative support, as later noted in the committee report. "It was made clear to the committee by those leaders that they were not committed to the plan proposed by the 1991 legislation and that they would cooperate fully in any reasonable alternative plan developed by this committee that would be more compatible with university objectives and priorities as well as with their own objectives. This view was supported by the sponsor of the legislation that would establish the Winston-Salem plan, and we welcome this spirit of cooperation."[22]

In March 1992, the Carson committee wrapped up its study. The committee did not support the idea of a separate Engineering and Science Research Center because of "the heavy costs that would be associated with the plans as presented to them." But it did agree that NC A&T should start doctoral programs in electrical and mechanical engineering, and that the collaboration in radiology research between Bowman Gray and NC State was successful and beneficial.[23]

"We believe that in the long term a stronger and expanded engineering presence in the region can be a significant force in economic development. We therefore recommend that the board of governors authorize the establishment of the 'Piedmont Triad Engineering Research and Technology Transfer Center' and that the legislation mandating the Piedmont Triad Graduate Research Institute be repealed."[24]

This new entity would include not only Wake Forest, UNC-G, and NC A&T, but UNC-Charlotte, which also had an engineering school, and Winston-Salem State, and would fall under the purview of the vice president for research of the University of North Carolina system. In a nod to both communities, the committee recommended that the new entity maintain two offices, one at the Graduate Center on the campus of Winston-Salem State and one at the School of Engineering at NC A&T. The legislature would be asked to provide $500,000 annually in start-up money for the first two years, augmented by $250,000 per year raised by the local communities.[25]

"We urge this plan be put into effect beginning in the summer of 1992...and that PTERTTC assume as its first responsibility the promotion and support of the cooperative radiology research effort at the Bowman Gray School of Medicine, and any other projects that it might be possible to finance with non-state funds."[26]

The UNC Board of Governors formally adopted the report and its recommendations a month later, but not before Greensboro officials made one last plea for the Engineering and Science Research Center. The Greensboro Development Corp. had invested $250,000 in a consultant to provide a detailed report on how to create and operate the center. Greensboro officials asked the governors to delay action pending his report, which was due to be completed by July 1. However, the governors were ready to move on. They would be willing to receive the report and consider amending their plans when the time came. But for now, Carson said, "They should think about melding themselves to our reality."[27]

In Winston-Salem, the community leaders pushing the engineering initiative pronounced themselves vindicated. The study had confirmed the need for graduate engineering in the Triad and had endorsed Bowman Gray's collaboration with NC State. The new doctoral programs authorized at NC A&T made it all the better. And now that the engineering initiative had the backing of the board of governors of the UNC system, their hand was strengthened before the General Assembly.

But the engineering push was only the means to an end: development of a technology-based economy. The recommendations in the report only increase the engineering resources that could draw technology companies to the area. When they came, they would need a place to put their facilities. It would be two more months before Hammer, Siler, George would complete its feasibility study, but from preliminary conversations with Vernon George, the technology advocates knew that their basic premise was sound. The area could support a research park. And, they thought, the Pinetree site offered the ideal setting. But while the community had been preoccupied with the Carson committee, Vernon George was coming to a very different conclusion.

5 A NEW VISION

Vernon George was not a yes man. His clients didn't always hear what they wanted him to say, and that was proving to be the case in Winston-Salem.

George and his firm, HSG, was part of the first wave of visionaries in the nascent field of urban planning who came to the fore as America used its postwar prosperity to rebuild itself after years of neglect during the Depression and World War II. Phillip Hammer founded Hammer and Company in Atlanta in 1954 after a career as a business consultant and as technical executive director of the agency that was the forerunner of the Atlanta metropolitan commission. The firm subsequently went through several name iterations as the business grew and partners came and left.[1]

Vernon George joined the company in 1963 after studying urban design and economics at Northwestern University, the University of Illinois, and the University of North Carolina. He began developing a specialty in research and technology parks in the early 1970s when he worked on a study for what became the Forrestal Center, a 2,200-acre research campus adjacent to Princeton University that would become the home to the university's world-leading Plasma Physics laboratory, private research and technology firms, and the necessary hotels, restaurants, and housing to support them.[2] In the years that followed he would conduct feasibility studies on almost 30 more research and technology projects, including assignments for Johns Hopkins University, the Medical College of Virginia, the University of Oklahoma Health Sciences, and University of Oregon Health Sciences.

George's collective experience, bolstered by his analysis of the market, convinced him that city leaders were off-base in their vision of a Triad version of Research Triangle Park.

The chamber's campaign to raise money to option the Pinetree site was the most obvious iteration of this mindset, but it had been there from the start. Back in 1989, when Maynard was promoting technology as a viable replacement for lost manufacturing jobs, he cited RTP as the model of his ultimate goal. "Although the community would like a 'quick fix' in regard to recruiting companies, a long-range plan is necessary when it comes to recruiting high-technology industries. *The Research Triangle Park has been around for a long time.*" (Emphasis added.)[3] Almost 20 years later, Doug Maynard and Gayle Anderson would freely confess their conventional thinking about where the park should be built. "When we heard the land was available," Maynard said, "she and I went out there and rode around the course. I thought it was a great idea. And we started approaching people to see if they would take it seriously."[4]

And, in fact, most community leaders did take it seriously. After a pitch to the Piedmont Triad Development Council, (comprised of the leaders of the largest employers in the Triad and chaired at the time by Wake Forest University President Tom Hearn) Jerry Long, a member, came up to Maynard and said, "I think it's a fantastic idea. I'll give you $50,000 right now if you want it."[5]

But the one person who was not taking it seriously was Vernon George. His initial feasibility study, turned in May 7, assured the chamber that the Triad could, in fact, support a research park. However, his contract with the chamber also called for a detailed site analysis.[6] George could have taken the path of least resistance and proceeded with an analysis of the Pinetree site that he knew his clients favored. However, he instinctively knew that this was the wrong place to start.

Years later, George would recall, "There were those in the community who felt if a middle of the region strategy worked in the Triangle it would work anywhere. My counsel was that the three-powerful-university, Triangle-region strategy worked *in spite of* substantial proximity disadvantages relative to other successful parks across the country."[7]

Maynard, Anderson, and the rest of Winston-Salem's technology advocates, having grown up with the Research Triangle Park, considered it the norm. But in fact, it was the exception to the rule. Duke University, NC State University, and the University of North Carolina at Chapel Hill all counted world-class researchers among their faculty, giving the Triangle region a powerful intellectual foundation for RTP. RTP also faced little competition in the late 1950s when it was established. In their global study of successful research parks, Willem Hulsink and Hans Dons noted that "few places in the United States or the world have a conglomeration of faculty and facilities comparable to that found in the Raleigh-Durham-Chapel Hill region" and that "very few research parks existed when RTP was first envisioned and began operations. The two best-known research sections were the Stanford Research Park in California and the Route 28 section around Boston in Massachusetts, and word of their success was spreading. But in the late 1950s, there was ample opportunity for other regions such as the Research Triangle, to replicate those successes."[8]

Even with these unique advantages, RTP was slow to gain traction. Although the park did not open until 1959, efforts to recruit tenants began in 1956.[9] Nonetheless, the park did not gain any tenant of consequence until 1965, when the U.S. Department of Health, Education and Welfare announced that it would build a $70 million Environmental Health Sciences Center in the park.[10] A few months later, IBM announced it would build a 56,000-square-foot research center in RTP. These twin announcements broke the ice. By 1969, 21 organizations had a research presence in RTP; by 1979, the park had 38 research tenants; and by 1989, 66.[11, 12]

RTP's success spurred a new movement among university communities to create research parks of their own. Prior to 1969, there were just 11 research parks in the United States. With the success of RTP, this number doubled (to 23) during the 1970s, and then came the explosion: 91 parks were started between 1980 and 1989.[13]

In one way or another, all these research parks were hoping

to mimic RTP's success. But their track record proved just how elusive the goal could be. Even as HSG was completing its feasibility study, two researchers at the University of North Carolina at Chapel Hill had found that half of all research parks that had been announced failed in the incubation stage, and that many of those that survived were converted to general business parks when they failed to attract a critical mass of research tenants.[14]

Vernon George, with his broader knowledge of research parks, realized that RTP was a special case and that, frankly, the Triad was not in a position to replicate its success. Any research park in the Triad would have to be closely tied to its intellectual engine to have a chance at succeeding. And so, a week after delivering his initial report, he began the process of tactfully weaning the technology advocates from their vision of building an RTP West.

On May 14, 1992, he sent an eight-page memo "to provide greater direction to the Steering Committee as to the relative levels of market demand at specific sites and on site strategy." In the memo, he presented five options in addition to Pinetree: A rural tract at the crossroads of U.S. 311 and N.C. 66; the Watkins Street area just west of downtown where Peters Creek Parkway crossed Business 40; an airport location near Interstate 40 and N.C. 68; the Piedmont Center at Miller and First streets just a few blocks from the medical school; and a site downtown centered on the old R.J. Reynolds Quality Assurance Building.[15]

"Research park market potentials are very much influenced by the location of the particular park site relative to supporting research activity. If direct ties to this research are to be important to many of the tenants, physical proximity and travel time convenience are important."[16]

And because "the overwhelming majority of cutting edge research in the Triad is being performed at the Bowman Gray School of Medicine...urban sites in close proximity to Bowman Gray could be expected to fare much better at attracting the research and technology-based tenant." In addition, George said, most research and technology tenants do not need a lot of space and cannot afford their own building. "For small tenants, an urban site in close proximity to the researchers and the full range of support services (post office, copy shop, office supply store etc.) is far preferable to an isolated suburban site."[17]

On the other hand, an urban park could not accommodate research and technology companies that outgrew their in-town location. And an urban site would not fare well in attracting information processing centers and technology-intensive man-ufacturing plants.

Because both types of uses – small research-based companies and large data processing/high-tech manufacturing facilities – factored in to the overall feasibility of building a research park, George posed "two key questions as it relates to moving ahead with Pinetree. First, do the absorption potentials justify the high land cost and substantial utility costs? And second, is the devel-opment of a park at Pinetree essential to capturing the informa-tion processing and technology-based potentials identified?"[18]

George supplied the answer to the second question: "Our research shows that these uses are often strongly attracted to freestanding sites and business park sites and do not exhibit a strong preference for freestanding research parks." As for the first question, only a detailed site analysis could tell. So the question now became: Which site should HSG pursue for its detailed site analysis? "I know the findings complicate the site strategy somewhat, but the important thing is that there remains strong potential for research park development."[19]

George's memo of May 14 gave pause in the rush to Pinetree, but it was not the only factor the Steering Committee had to consider. It was still having trouble raising money to option the Pinetree site. And even though the committee envi-sioned one research park to serve the Triad – and had freely shared HSG's preliminary feasibility study with other commu-nities in the Triad – civic leaders in Greensboro had shown that they were inclined to go their own way.

And in the midst of the study, RJR Tobacco – too cash strapped to harbor any ambitions for its obsolete downtown factories – decided to donate them to Forsyth County and take the tax write-off. The county commissioners were studying what to do with them.[20]

With all these factors up in the air, the chamber's Technology Committee instructed George to put his follow-up study on hold until they had a better idea of where Greensboro and the county were headed with their respective studies.[21] And then Reynolds made another move that essentially decided the issue of where to put the research park. On Oct. 1, 1992, the company sent Dick Janeway at the medical school a letter announcing that it was going to sell its Quality Assurance Building at the corner of Chestnut and Belews streets. "If the building is not sold to a commercial user, the company is considering selling the building to a not-for-profit organization for $1 million, which is substantially below market value."[22] An identical letter was sent to Winston-Salem State University.[23]

The Quality Assurance Building was a two-story, beige-brick building at the southern end of the phalanx of Reynolds factories that defined the eastern edge of downtown. It was in the heart of one site George was proposing for the research park. Reynolds had spent $1.75 million to put up the building in 1951 to match the R&D efforts of its rival brands.[24] When completed, it was one of the most up-to-date laboratory facilities of its kind, comprising 51,000 square feet of laboratory space, 30,000 square feet of office space, and 21,000 square feet housing the heating, cooling, and ventilation systems the laboratories required.[25]

Most of the research at the building had since been moved to Reynolds' Bowman Gray Research Center, next to its Whitaker Park plant on the north side of town. And with Reynolds having just donated its downtown factories to the county, the Quality Assurance Building was an asset the company no longer needed.

In a request for proposals dated Oct. 1, 1992, the company asked each interested non-profit to reply by Oct. 30, describing:
- How it would use the building, especially its laboratory space.
- How it would benefit by having the building, both in the short and long term.
- How it would pay for the building.
- How its ownership of the building would benefit downtown.[26]

Although the RFP was sent to Winston-Salem State as well as the medical school, it clearly was tailored to the medical school's needs. Reynolds' decision to close its manufacturing complex had created a void downtown. Something was needed to replace the lost jobs and fill the empty acres, and Reynolds – harking back to its original notion of using the area for an applied research park – wanted that something to be the proposed research park.[27] Through Haver, the company knew that HSG had suggested a downtown location. Presenting the medical school with an offer too good to refuse was one way to ensure that it happened.

The medical school readily took the bait. With the agreement of university President Tom Hearn and the board of trustees, Janeway sent back a proposal that described how the medical school would use the building to fulfill a grab-bag of needs, starting with the newly created Center for Research on Human Nutrition and Chronic Disease Prevention. With the building in hand, Bowman Gray could accelerate the timetable for launching research at the center. Otherwise, such research – and the jobs it would create – would await completion of a new building several years hence.[28]

In addition, the wet lab space in the building could bring under one roof the medical school's largest and best-known research program in cardiovascular health; as the program had grown, it had spread out here and there as space on the Hawthorne Hill campus became available. Wet lab space could also allow the school to create a transgenic animal facility "that will become the focal point for the transfer of basic research into gene therapy for human disease and that will represent another important recruiting tool to attract high-tech industry to the Triad." Some of the office space in the building would support these research programs. In the space left over, the medical school proposed to house the Piedmont Triad Engineering Research Center, with some reserved "for headquarters of a proposed downtown research park."[29]

To further sweeten its bid, the medical school proposed that once the Nutrition Center's building on the Hawthorne campus was completed, some of the space it had used in the Quality

Assurance Building could be set aside for "any start-up technology-dependent company that requires wet lab space."[30]

The medical school's bid met all of Reynolds' criteria, but
the company, mindful of its public relations, asked Bowman
Gray to ensure that Winston-Salem State had no designs on the
building. The net result was a revised proposal, submitted Nov.
23, 1992, that set aside 5,000 square feet of laboratory space
and 3,800 square feet of administrative space for WSSU faculty
research and undergraduate laboratory programs and its Life
Science education program.[31]

RJR's Quality Assurance Building in 1961.
Photo by Frank Jones, courtesy of Winston-Salem Journal

Throughout the summer, Hammer, Siler, George had been
on hold. Its contract called for preparation of a detailed site
analysis of one site for a research park, but the Steering Committee had postponed making that decision. By the end of
October, circumstances dictated the answer: Greensboro was
not interested in participating in a Triad-wide research park;
the Steering Committee was still lacking money to option
the Pinetree site; and the medical school was about to buy
the Quality Assurance Building. The research park would be
downtown.

Two other sites – the Piedmont Center and the Watkins

Street area – were closer to the Bowman Gray campus, but both had drawbacks: The Piedmont Center – the old headquarters of Piedmont Airlines – was hemmed in by existing development in an expensive part of town, which could inhibit future expansion. And the Watkins Street area was steeply sloped and would be expensive to develop. Even without these drawbacks, other factors dictated that the downtown site was the best, including its easy access to highways, its visibility, the availability of business support services such as printers, and the fact that some of the land was already in public ownership. And finally, putting the research park downtown would promote downtown revitalization and assist the county in its efforts to redevelop the Reynolds Tobacco factories it now owned.[32]

With its marching orders in hand, HSG went to work, and in January 1993 it filed its final report, laying out a 15-year development plan for the research park.

In all, HSG estimated that the area could support as much as 440,000 square feet of new research and development space in addition to the existing Quality Assurance Building – enough to serve the park for 15 years, given its absorption projections. As envisioned by HSG, the completed park would comprise four new buildings adjacent to the Quality Assurance Building, arranged around a landscaped plaza on the southwest corner of First and Chestnut streets that would serve as a focal point for the park.[33]

The first phase of the construction, of course, would be redevelopment of the Quality Assurance Building. HSG endorsed the medical school's plans to temporarily house the nutrition center in the building, but it did not concur with the school's plans to use the rest of the lab space for the cardiovascular program and to allocate space for R&D start-ups only after the nutrition center decamped. "The availability of functional laboratory space is a valuable asset in the marketing of research park space. The high cost of laboratory construction often places lab space beyond the reach of small companies, particularly start-up companies in the process of commercializing an innovation. The ability to offer finished lab space at market or below-market rents would be invaluable in recruiting and assisting technology-based companies."[34]

"Other Bowman Gray entities" (i.e. the cardiovascular program) could move in once the nutrition center moved out, HSG recommended. "Of course, the exact terms of such an agreement would need to be negotiated with Bowman Gray, but we would strongly recommend a sale of the building by RJR to Bowman Gray with a provision that the medical school make available a minimum of 15,000 square feet for research park tenancy."[35]

To map out the rest of the park, HSG brought in Wallace Roberts & Todd, an urban design and architectural firm. Phase 2 was to be a three-story building with 90,000 square feet spanning the northern side of First Street between Church and Chestnut; Phase 3 would bring 150,000 square feet in a five-story building at the end of Chestnut Street along Business 40; Phases 4 and 5 would comprise a four-story L-shaped building with 200,000 square feet wrapping around the park on the block south of First Street between Church and Chestnut. Parking would be provided in surface lots between the Quality Assurance Building and the railroad tracks east of the site. Later a parking deck would be built with Phase 5 on the block south of City Hall between Main and Church streets.[36]

Five pages of accompanying design guidelines were provided "to create a visually cohesive precinct, which is identifiable in the city as a unique and special place.... Therefore the individual buildings should have similar design characteristics, much as does a great university campus." Visual cues should come from the existing buildings downtown and the historic Reynolds Tobacco factory No. 256, and yet "the buildings should aspire to expressions of the science that is taking place within them."

To accomplish this, the appendix included detailed guidance on building locations, heights, entrances, materials and façade patterns, "roofscapes," signs, and maintenance. Nothing was left to chance.

Plans on paper mean nothing without the money to make them real. HSG addressed this with a financial analysis that included a pro forma cash flow projection, with the provision that bringing the site to market would require a large initial investment. Land acquisition alone would cost an estimated $1.7 million, and this figure was assuming that the prison site owned by Forsyth County would be donated to the park as a cleared site. Streetscape improvements were estimated at $3.43 million and the public plaza was estimated at $900,000. A cash-flow analysis indicated that the cost of the buildings themselves could be recovered by rents over 30 years.[37]

However, the park could not run itself. "Successful development of a research park requires a skilled and dedicated staff," HSG noted, capable of soliciting and managing financial support, marketing the park, negotiating land acquisition and partnerships with private developers to put up the buildings, overseeing park development, and managing public and community relations. "This intensive and diverse work program is not something which can be handled on a part-time basis by staff with other responsibilities and deadlines. It demands a separate organization whose effectiveness is judged solely on the basis of progress in developing the research park. At a minimum, the research park organization should have a full-time executive director with appropriate clerical and administrative support." The cost? HSG estimated it at $327,000 annually.[38]

The net result: Over the first 12 years of operations the park would run a deficit every year, ranging from a low of $17,000 in year 10, up to more than $6.1 million in year 11 when a parking deck would have to be built. Over all 12 years, the cumulative deficit totaled $18.62 million. And these figures did not include the capital costs of the buildings, which were assumed to be revenue neutral.[39]

In other words, "as with research parks around the country, the slow pace of research park development makes private development infeasible. Public or private non-profit funding of land acquisition, streetscaping, plaza landscaping and/or structured parking will be required to make the research park financially feasible."[40]

HSG's 82-page report gave the community the road map it sought for transforming the economy, not just of Winston-Salem, but potentially of the entire Triad. The feasibility study had revealed that Greensboro had assets that could contribute to the effort. But Vernon George also realized that he could not force "Triadism" on a constituency that was not yet willing to act regionally (as amply demonstrated by the dust-up over the Piedmont Triad Graduate Research Institute). The undercurrent of intercity rivalry within the Triad precluded the notion that Greensboro's leaders would support a research park in Winston-Salem. And yet their support would be necessary in securing state support.

The solution, he suggested, was for Greensboro to develop its own research park, drawing upon research coming out of the Engineering and Science Research Center, once UNC-Greensboro and NC A&T got it up and running. And then, with those two parks on line, the original concept of a large, centrally located technology park eventually might be warranted to accommodate manufacturing spin-offs.[41] Finally, as a gesture toward High Point, he suggested that High Point look into developing a small research park that would work in tandem with the furniture industry.[42] But in private, George was frank about the High Point suggestion: "The purpose really was to preserve the regional support for the park effort relative to state funding."[43]

But the first order of business was to start the downtown research park in Winston-Salem. HSG gave the community a vision and a game plan. But it would not take long before reality changed it.

6 THE JAILHOUSE CAMPUS

While HSG spent the fall of 1992 finalizing its report, the technology advocates in Winston-Salem were preparing for yet another legislative effort to advance their agenda. The 1991 General Assembly had authorized creation of the Piedmont Triad Graduate Research Institute, but had not allotted it any money. With adoption of the Carson Report, city leaders agreed to let the institute be supplanted by the Piedmont Triad Engineering Research Center. This left the city in the position of having one organization – still on the books as a matter of state law – eligible to receive state money, while the new organization had yet to be recognized or financed by the state.

Local officials were now referring to the center by acronym PTERC, which they pronounced as "pea-turk." Forsyth legislators had introduced a bill to create and fund PTERC during the short session in the summer of 1992, but it had failed to win unanimous support and died in committee.[1] That effort had been something of a long shot, given the legislature's long-standing preference to limit the scope of the short session to updates of existing programs.

The new legislature that would convene in January offered a much more realistic opportunity, and once again the city turned to Rep. Lyons Gray to spearhead their approach. With the concurrence of administrators with the University of North Carolina, Gray planned to introduce a new bill to authorize PTERC and provide it with $500,000 a year for two years. Concurrently, the UNC Board of Governors would request a like amount in the expansion budget they submitted to the General Assembly.[2]

With more time to prepare, the advocates devised a 13-point

strategy that included giving tours of the medical school and its technology-related initiatives to key legislators, and holding a series of briefings to secure the unanimous support of the Triad Legislative Caucus. The strategy also reached out into the business community. Lobbyists for local corporations would be briefed on the initiative and asked to support it. Local business executives acquainted with legislators outside the Triad would be asked to write letters to them in support, as would members of the UNC Board of Governors. Finally, Gov. Jim Hunt would be briefed and asked for his support.[3]

The most difficult part of the strategy called for securing the support of business and academic leaders in Greensboro. Over the summer, Ed David, a consultant hired by the Greensboro Development Corporation, had turned in his report on how to create and operate the proposed Engineering and Science Research Center. It laid out an ambitious vision of a Triad-based center of excellence that – contrary to the recommendations in the Carson report – would operate as an independent entity serving and directed by the two Greensboro campuses. After reviewing the study, the GDC organized a series of presentations on the study, including one in October attended by Doug Maynard and Gayle Anderson.[4]

In a memo afterwards to Wake Forest President Tom Hearn and Bowman Gray Dean Dick Janeway, Maynard was frank in his evaluation: "Although (the study) is poorly done, some parts of it are good.... The GDC has done a commendable job of paring down the study (and) wants to develop a program to implement those aspects...that make sense.... Chancellors Moran (UNC-G) and Fort (NC A&T) were at the meeting I attended in Greensboro. I believe they still favor the ESRC proposal and hope that somehow it will happen. However, the organizers of the meetings told me afterwards that prospects for the plan are not promising. They believe that PTERC should be the initial step and that, since the action in the Triad is primarily within the medical school, that was the logical place to begin." [5]

While this was encouraging, Maynard warned that opposition from UNC-G and NC A&T could spell trouble once the bill was in the legislature. "I still believe that Drs. Moran and Fort will have to be convinced that the ESRC won't happen and that NC State University must have a very active role in whatever engineering and computer science graduate research and educational programs develop in the Triad."[6] Toward that end, Maynard asked Pete Santago to approach his old friend Harold Martin, the dean of NC A&T's engineering school. It was "necessary and appropriate," Santago wrote Martin, "to solicit your comments and recommendations" regarding the strategy for establishing PTERC, the GDC study, and "other matters pertaining to the development of graduate engineering programs in the Piedmont Triad."[7]

As a backstop, Gray agreed to introduce a bill to provide $500,000 a year for two years to the Piedmont Triad Graduate Research Institute, with the tacit agreement that the money would be turned over to PTERC if the upcoming session again failed to act.[8] On the Senate side, Ted Kaplan would introduce an identical bill.[9]

Concurrent with these efforts, the Downtown Development Corporation, a non-profit alliance of Winston-Salem organizations, turned to the task of finding money to develop the research park. With the agreement of all parties, initial responsibility for oversight and development of the research park had been given to the corporation in the fall of 1992 as the HSG study took shape and it became clear that Vernon George would recommend a downtown site for the park.

Although local governments, corporations, and foundations would be asked to contribute, the amount necessary to complete just the first phase of the park was more than they could bear. However, the legislature's authorization of the Piedmont Triad Graduate Research Institute during the 1991 session – coupled with plans to house the institute at the park – gave city leaders the grounds to seek a capital appropriation from the General Assembly. As with the effort to secure money for PTERC, the legislative effort for the park would have to be a Triad-wide initiative. Of course, Guilford County legislators were not about to support a "Triad" bill that solely helped Forsyth County, so the request to the legislature would have to include something for Greensboro. That something, the Greensboro Development Corporation decided, should be a Manufacturing Application and Education Center at NC A&T. Greensboro leaders viewed the center as one of the more feasible aspects of their consultant's report on the Engineering and Science Research Center.

Philosophically, Winston-Salem had no objection to bringing Greensboro into the effort. HSG's initial feasibility study was based on the potential of the entire Triad – not just Winston-Salem – to support a research park. And from the start, Winston-Salem advocates had seen the research initiative as one that would serve that entire Triad, as demonstrated by the chamber's effort to secure the Pinetree site. Development of a manufacturing center at NC A&T also conformed with HSG's recommendation that Greensboro create a park to take advantage of research coming out of that university.

But it did complicate the legislative effort, which was put under the umbrella of the Piedmont Triad Development Corporation, a loose alliance of business and civic advocacy groups that worked on Triad-wide initiatives. The backing of the Piedmont Triad Development Corporation would give more standing to the appropriation request when it went before the General Assembly. But it also required far more cooperation between multiple groups whose agendas – as illustrated by the holdouts for the Engineering and Science Research Center – did not always jibe.

With the need for added coordination and the time it took to secure the approval of multiple entities, the final legislative strategy was not hammered out until the end of March 1993, bumping up against an April 1 deadline for introducing bills for the session. In its final form, the Triad requested $16 million in 1993-1995 biennial budget – $8 million for each year. Ten million dollars in capital spending would fund development of the downtown research park in Winston-Salem ($2 million each year), provide matching funds for a $10 million federal grant to develop the Manufacturing Application and Education Center ($2.5 million per year) and allocate $500,000 a year in seed money to start a new Triad organization that would oversee the parks' development and coordinate their activities. Concurrently, $6 million requested for the UNC Board of Governors budget would finance the Piedmont Triad Engineering Research Center for two years ($3.4 million) and allocate $1.3 million each year to NC A&T, UNC-G, and Winston-Salem State for accelerated development of graduate programs in engineering, science, and computer science, respectively.[10]

To build support for the request (and to address lingering public confusion about the two initiatives), Maynard sent a nine-page article to the Winston-Salem Journal making the case for both PTERC and the research park. Although the Journal did not publish the article, it did prompt a Sunday column by John Gates, the editor of the Journal editorial page, supporting them. Gates made light of the alphabet-soup shorthand for the many entities involved (including, but not limited to, PTERC, PTGRI, ESRC, DDC, GDC, and PTRP) noting that they alone "are enough to glaze the eyes and numb the mind." But overall, he supported the initiatives and agreed that the vision of bringing engineering and technology to the Triad was needed to ensure the future health of the regional economy.[11]

While the legislature took up the funding request, the medical school finalized the purchase of the Quality Assurance Building from R.J. Reynolds. The school's bid to Reynolds had promised a "major medical school research presence" in the building. But it was having trouble making good on this promise. In its bid, the school said it would house the Center for Nutrition and Chronic Disease Prevention downtown while the new building on campus was completed. But federal support for the center had stalled.

As a fallback, the school turned to its research group studying hypertension and vascular disease, led by Dr. Carlos Ferrario. Ferrario was one of the medical school's star researchers, a native of Argentina who had received his postgraduate training in cardiology at the University of Goteborg in Sweden before going to the Cleveland Clinic, where he was chair of the Department of Brain and Vascular Research. In

1992, Dick Janeway lured him to Bowman Gray with carte blanche to establish a new Hypertension and Vascular Disease Center as he saw fit. Ferrario's arrival – and the federal research grants he brought with him – had considerably boosted the medical school's standing both in reputation and in the "NIH derby" of funded research, and that gave him considerable clout. "Carlos Ferrario was an internationally recognized icon in hypertension research, and we stole the whole group from the Cleveland Clinic," Janeway said, "and we wanted to keep them happy."[12]

Janeway was hoping that Ferrario would be attracted by the opportunity to move into his own building, with laboratories customized for each researcher's needs. Ferrario was willing to entertain the idea. But most of his researchers had no interest in moving downtown, and Janeway understood their reluctance. "There is some hazard in accumulating too much of the basic research on a satellite campus," Janeway said, "because the important thing about biotech research is the translational research. You have to do things with the basic sciences that have clinical implications, that can translate into improvements in patient care. And if you're not on the main campus where the patient care is being done, it's harder to maintain that contact."[13]

But the move downtown was also proving a hard sell for more elementary reasons. The building would have none of the easy access to the cafeteria, post office, and other amenities on Hawthorne Hill that simplified the work day. Worse yet, the Quality Assurance Building was a lonely outpost in a desolate corner of downtown, surrounded by abandoned Reynolds factories, a lumber yard, and the old county jail, all framed by desolate parking lots punctuated by weeds rooted in the cracked asphalt. The Quality Assurance Building might represent the start of the future research park – a vision, it should be noted, that was not uniformly shared on the Hawthorne campus – but at the moment, it could only be seen as a very dubious location.

Nonetheless, the school had just handed Reynolds a million dollars for the building, and it needed to put something in there. Janeway canvassed his department heads and found that

Jim Smith, the chair of the Department of Physiology and Pharmacology, was willing to consider a move. "I didn't have a lot of space and we were very successful in gaining NIH dollars and we were busting at the seams," Smith said. "And the possibility of getting more space on the Hawthorne campus was remote."[14] Given these circumstances, Smith was willing to consider a move.

In late May, Smith and several of his senior faculty toured the building. "We looked at the possibilities and then it was an issue of, 'What would the institution do to remodel it to meet the needs of our faculty?'" There was also the issue of selling the rest of the faculty on the move. "We had a committee of faculty talk to all the faculty to see what would be necessary to make it a win-win opportunity for them." It soon became apparent that gaining new labs, customized for the specific needs of each researcher, would go a long way toward gaining their support. Smith and a faculty committee spent the next two months putting together a detailed proposal for moving the department, including how the space would be assigned, what equipment was needed, and what physical changes would be necessary to accommodate their research.[15]

"We submitted the bid (to the medical school), and that's when negotiations began," Smith said. "They said, 'This looks good, but we have to discuss some things.'... People wanted brand new lab counters, which was one of the things we compromised on. It ends up there are ways of taking older counters and coating them and they look brand new. And they could use most of the existing cabinetry, and use most of the old hoods. Where we were requesting new things, the institution utilized things already here that could be reconditioned to a like-new state."[16]

In all, it took about three months to negotiate the details. Even then, Smith had misgivings. "I had a significant amount of anxiety," he said. "I had provided leadership for the department and was risking my credibility if we moved down here and it ended up being a bad situation.... I might have been put in a circumstance where I might have to step down as chair. But I considered the alternative, and the alternative was: Sit there land-locked and not be able to grow our programs. And I had faculty who were being more and more successful in bringing in dollars for research, which means you have to have more people and space and equipment. The future welfare of the department was best met by taking this chance."[17]

With the terms of the move settled, the head of the school physical plant inspected the building and provided an estimate of how much it would cost. When he concluded that the aging boilers and mechanical systems would have to be replaced, the price jumped another $2.5 million.[18]

The building make-over included the best security system available, including video monitors at all the building doors and a card-access system to each hallway. These measures were to ward off not only would-be burglars who might be tempted by the computers and other expensive equipment in the building, but also any animal-rights activists who from time to time protested the use of animals in the department's research.[19] To reduce the sense of isolation and facilitate collaboration with researchers on the Hawthorne campus and elsewhere, the building was connected to the high-speed network that tied the medical school to the state microwave network.

It took about a year to renovate the building for the department. On the first Monday in October 1994, Jim Smith became the first to move. "The institution stood behind all the promises it made, but I have to say, my faculty were still reluctant. It was going to take about two and a half months to move the whole department."

It was a tricky situation. Smith was not going to force anyone to move, and yet having spent millions to buy and renovate the building, the prospect of moving downtown was no longer academic.[20] "Then," Smith said, "a few people moved into the new labs, and their enthusiasm became infectious. Those people on the waiting list became anxious. When I agreed to come, I thought it might take a year and a half before faculty might begin to think that they made the right move. I was unbelievably surprised that, two weeks after we began the move, people were so enthusiastic.... People who were waiting to move here were visiting and saying, 'Wow, I can't wait to get in here.'...

"It ended up that what we gained was far more than the conveniences that we were giving up. That became very obvious, probably after 90 days, when people were all saying, 'Oh, this was a good thing.'" This would be borne out in the decade that followed, as the department watched its NIH-sponsored research more than triple, from $5 million a year in 1995 to $16 million by the start of 2006.[21]

And as it turned out, security was never an issue, Smith said. "Once we got down here, we realized there was nothing around us to attract any individuals who might want to prey on us." Moreover, the presence of the county jail ensured that police officers and sheriff's deputies were routinely in the area. Soon, wags in the department were referring to their workplace as "the jailhouse campus."

Although the researchers with the Department of Physiology and Pharmacology occupied the lion's share of the Quality Assurance building, they were not alone. In putting together their bid, the department allocated space for Winston-Salem State University and for the Piedmont Triad Engineering Research Center.

For Winston-Salem State, the 3,000 square feet set aside in the building for its computer science and allied health faculty represented an important toe-hold in the vision of creating a full-blown research park essentially next door to its main campus.[22]

Additionally, WSSU's presence, along with that of PTERC, gave legitimacy to the claim that the building was not merely an outpost of the medical school, but rather the start of a multi-institution research park. The value of this distinction was borne out during the 1993 legislative session, when the General Assembly took up the Piedmont Triad Development Corporation's funding request.

As expected, the two-year, $16 million funding request did not survive intact, given the competition for money in a tight budget year. Instead of the $1.7 million per year the Triad requested for operating PTERC, the UNC Board of Governors' budget request included just $500,000 a year. And as it turned out, not even that lesser amount was approved.

The capital appropriation for the research park, however, fared better. Here, the efforts of state Sens. Ted Kaplan of Forsyth County and George Daniel, the chairman of the Triad legislative caucus, paid off, in no small part because both sat on the Senate Appropriations Committee and were in a position to make things happen. Daniel was the committee chairman, and Kaplan was the chairman of its subcommittee on capital expenditure. Their challenge was finding an acceptable channel to deliver the money, Kaplan said. Given the tight budget, any effort to send state money to a private organization stood little chance of success.[23]

The proximity of the Forsyth County Jail (in the foreground) led some medical center personnel to refer to the Quality Assurance Building as "the jailhouse campus."

Photo courtesy of Winston-Salem Journal

Winston-Salem State's participation in the park, however minimal, provided the cover they needed. With the assent of Daniel, Kaplan inserted – in the closing hours of the session as bills were being rushed to the floor for a vote – $3 million in the capital budget for the UNC Board of Governors, earmarked for

Winston-Salem State as "state support for the cooperative effort of NC A&T, UNC-Greensboro, North Carolina State University in the establishment of research parks in the Winston-Salem area."[24]

What happened next was a testimony to the cooperative spirit that had taken hold in Winston-Salem's effort to transform its economy. With the money being channeled through Winston-Salem State, that institution could easily have diverted a portion for some other, unfunded need, or taken a cut as an "administrative expense" for handing the money. However, Maynard received a call from Chancellor Cleon Thompson the day after the General Assembly approved the appropriation. "He said, 'Doug, we know what that money is for and you will get every penny of it.'"[25]

Thompson, in fact, had supported the request all the way through the legislative process. "We felt that having this facility in close proximity to the institution would be a great benefit to the students," he said. "They would be able to have internships with these small businesses. We knew it was a way to help educate our students. These companies could provide more hands-on lab resources than we could provide as an institution." In addition, he said, "There were some very dirty businesses – the lumber yard and some other plants – in the area that produced a lot of dust. And we were trying to put clean industries in that area. We wanted to improve the view of the campus."[26]

The $3 million – the actual figure was $3,026,000 – constituted a good start, but given the lack of funding for PTERC, it was not enough to pursue both visions. In September 1993, as Jim Smith was wrapping up his negotiations with the medical school over renovations to the Quality Assurance Building, a committee comprising Doug Maynard, Don Haver, Gayle Anderson, Jack Steelman, Pete Santago, and Wes Snyder put together a proposal that envisioned augmenting the state appropriation with $1.5 million in private contributions that Haver volunteered to solicit. These private contributions, along with $817,000 of the state appropriation, would be used to activate PTERC. The remaining $2.2 million would be used to pay for the renovations in the Quality Assurance Building for the space to be occupied by WSSU faculty, PTERC, and the research park administrative offices.[27]

But within a month, this plan fizzled out. With the economy struggling, Haver soon realized that he would not be able to raise anywhere close to $1.5 million. By early October, the committee had moved on to Plan B: Put PTERC on hold, make it the community's top legislative priority for the next session of the General Assembly, and use the state appropriation to move forward with the research park in accordance with the development plan laid out by Hammer, Siler, George.[28]

In a letter to Chancellor Thompson, Maynard noted that half a million dollars of this money would go toward upfitting offices for WSSU, the research park administration, and PTERC so that "the building will be ready for the immediate start-up of PTERC once operating funds are available." Of the remaining $2.5 million, $2 million would be allocated for land acquisition and site improvements, and the rest spent on planning, environmental studies, engineering, legal fees, and park marketing.[29]

Three months after this was decided, however, Winston-Salem officials faced a new public relations problem. Jasper Memory, the vice president for research for the University of North Carolina system, was none too pleased with an appropriation that seemed to benefit a project being driven by Wake Forest University. His impression was understandable: Wake Forest was three months into its renovations of the Quality Assurance Building for Jim Smith's department, and the university had been the driving force behind PTERC, which was also to be housed in the building. Memory's ire was further aroused by the furtive manner in which the appropriation was slipped in at the last minute. Perhaps cued by the original, failed plan to use the bulk of the money to renovate the Quality Assurance Building, Memory went public with his concerns. "If public funds are going to be used, it seems appropriate that the public university system should be the recipient of the money and the central player in any state-funded project. The ambivalence that we feel is that, all things being equal, if the state of North Carolina is going to give state funds for higher education, it seems to be more appropriate for the money to go to a public institution rather than for the state to give a large portion to a private institution."[30]

Notwithstanding the fact that the money actually had been appropriated to a public institution (a ploy that Memory quickly saw through), Winston-Salem officials had moved on to Plan B well before Memory raised his objections. Thompson said the arrangement was a bargain. "It gives our faculty an opportunity to work in pure research labs that we do not have here on campus." Kaplan called the appropriation a stimulant for economic development. "It was creating a facility that would create a lot of capital investment." Rep. Lyons Gray, the head of the Forsyth delegation, responded with a verbal shrug. "The capital bill was one of the last bills, and those who were still working hard were lucky." Ultimately, Memory's objection went nowhere. Senior UNC administrators knew better than to bite the hands of the legislators who appropriated their budget, and the controversy quickly fizzled.[31]

With a game plan in place, money in hand, and renovation of the Quality Assurance Building underway, New Year's Day 1994 arrived with a sense that many years of effort were beginning to pay off. And in truth, the vision of a downtown research park was now closer than ever. But a dispassionate analysis showed that the projects underway amounted not so much to a research park as to an extension of Bowman Gray Medical School, and to a much lesser extent, Winston-Salem State. The research park community leaders envisioned would be a place where high-tech companies could take root and grow. Toward that end, HSG had recommended reserving speculative space in the Quality Assurance Building for private high-tech tenants. This recommendation had gone by the wayside. It would prove to be an expensive oversight.

7 IF YOU BUILD IT, WILL THEY COME?

It was too good to be true. For six years, a cadre of Winston-Salem visionaries had been working to create a research park that would transform the city's economy. And now, even before the park was ready, fate was offering them a chance for early vindication.

It happened during August 1994. The research park was still largely a paper entity. The medical school's Department of Physiology and Pharmacology was three months away from moving to the Quality Assurance Building, which had been renamed the Piedmont Triad Community Research Center. The master plan for developing the park would not be completed for another month.

And yet, here was Smith & Nephew Dyonics Inc., a world leader in arthroscopic surgical equipment, making plans to check out the still-embryonic research park as a possible relocation site for its corporate headquarters. The company, according to press accounts, wanted a building with 300,000 square feet that would employ as many as 500 people. Moreover, Dyonics wanted a location where it would "be able to forge relationships with universities doing engineering and medical research, particularly one that would be nearby."[1]

North Carolina Gov. Jim Hunt was actively courting Dyonics and the company was considering not only Winston-Salem, but Raleigh and Charlotte, too. Jacksonville, Fla., was also said to be in consideration, and Massachusetts had put together an attractive package of incentives to convince Dyonics to stay put.[2]

Winston-Salem leaders knew that Dyonics' interest was premature, but that didn't stop them from putting their best foot forward: If Dyonics decided to come to Winston-Salem, they agreed, the research park would custom-build a new headquarters to the company's specifications. PTERC, too, was in the early days, and it would be easy to steer its efforts to support Dyonics' needs. And of course, the medical center could provide all the surgical support the company could want.

Even though it was a long shot, the city's leadership planned to put on a full-court press when Dyonics came to town. Gayle Anderson would organize a visit to the research park site, accompanied by Don Haver, the chairman of the Downtown Development Corp.; Bob Leak, the chamber's business recruiter; Jack Steelman, the city's downtown development director and staff director of the Downtown Development Corp.; and Bob Brown of GBQC Architects, the firm developing the master plan for the research park.[3]

Next would come a visit with the leaders of the PTERC and the engineering initiative, including Pete Santago and Harold Martin, the dean of engineering at NC A&T. This would be followed by a visit with the medical school's group working on minimally invasive surgery, which depended on arthroscopic surgical equipment. There would be courtesy calls on Dick Janeway and Tom Hearn, and a meal with the city's leadership, to include Mayor Martha Wood, state Sen. Ted Kaplan, Wachovia CEO Bud Baker, RJR CEO Jim Johnson, and others.[4]

The site visit came off as planned. GBQC unveiled a hastily revised master plan with a 300,000-square-foot building on the parcel between Belews Street and Business 40, giving it prime exposure. At the medical school, the Dyonics delegation observed a surgery in progress, during which the surgeon spoke with them about use of their products and how he would work with Dyonics to improve them.[5]

Alas, it was not to be. In the end, inertia – combined with Massachusetts' incentive package – convinced Dyonics to stay put. Nonetheless, it was a tantalizing hint of what might be. As far as the research park's proponents were concerned, just the fact that the city had a research park – even one that essentially existed only on paper at this point – had been enough to validate its founding premise. Without the medical school and the research park, Dyonics never would have considered Winston-Salem.[6]

Even before Dyonic's flirtation with Winston-Salem, the Downtown Development Corp. had handed oversight of the park to a new committee with the sole responsibility of shepherding the research park to completion. The Piedmont Triad Research Park Management Committee comprised many of the same players, among them Doug Maynard, Gayle Anderson, Don Haver, Jack Steelman, and Fred Nordenholz. Other members represented entities that the park would need as it developed: Bob Leak, the president of Winston-Salem Business Inc; Patrick Diamond, the district manager of Duke Power; David Swann of Wachovia Bank; and David Park of Southern National Bank; Graham Pervier, the Forsyth County manager; and William Davis, a partner in the Womble Carlyle Sandridge & Rice law firm. Representing academia, in addition to Maynard, were Joanne Ruhland, the planning institutional coordinator for the medical center; Everett Witherspoon, the vice chancellor for academic affairs at Winston-Salem State; Robert Swofford, the chemistry department chairman at Wake Forest; Sam Grogg, the dean of the filmmaking school at the School of the Arts; and Harold Martin, the dean of the engineering school at NC A&T.[7]

The committee would be responsible for executing the master plan for park development. This presented some formidable challenges. The committee did not yet control all the land for the park that the master plan assumed would be part of the park, let alone have the money for the spec building needed to lure the first tenants. It had to find money to hire a park staff (beyond the $100,000 that the Chamber of Commerce had set aside), recruit and hire the park staff, find money for the required infrastructure improvements and public spaces, draft protective covenants to protect the park as it developed, and raise at least three years of operating funds for the park.[8]

Of the $3.1 million the state had allocated, roughly $1.8 million remained. The committee members knew from the start that this $3.1 million would not be enough to do the job, but they soon learned that, in fact, it was only half of what it would take. A revised budget prepared by Jack Steelman put the capital cost of developing the park at $6.26 million. Of the additional $3.16 million needed, $2.76 million was needed for land acquisition and site preparation.[9]

In the wake of Dyonics' visit, Vernon George proposed a more systematic approach for attracting tenants by conducting a marketing relationship "census." This census would identify "the relationships which members of the Winston-Salem community have with individuals, businesses and institutions around the country and the world which could lead to tenancy in the park."[10]

The census was an exercise in organized common sense: The committee would cast a wide net among business and community leaders, researchers at the medical school, and professors at the universities, asking them to identify potential tenants with whom they had a personal, business, or professional relationship. A census form would identify the prospect's name, organization, and contact information, and describe the nature of the relationship with the prospect. The "originator" of the marketing lead would indicate why this person was included in the marketing census, whether the prospect's organization was considering a new facility, whether the prospect had other relationships with people in Winston-Salem or North Carolina, and whether other researchers in Winston-Salem might be of interest to this prospect. The originator would recommend the best way to approach the prospect, and the best way to follow up that initial contact. Ideally, every person who identified a relationship with a prospect would be asked to make the initial contact. However, George knew from experience that many researchers are averse to making sales pitches, so he included contact options for every originator's comfort zone, ranging from initiating the first telephone call and taking an active part in the recruitment, to simply identifying the prospect and leaving the rest up to others.[11]

The marketing census was a necessary first step toward populating the park, but there remained the issue of where to put any tenants that might be found. Steelman's revised estimate of $6.26 million to complete the park did not include the cost of putting up a building for new tenants. Vernon George, aware of the need to have space available to show prospects, had recommended that the city fill this need in the short term by setting aside some spec space during renovation of the Quality Assurance Building. This had not been done, in part because of the questions that had been raised about the state's allocation for the research park. Would Dyonics have given Winston-Salem more serious consideration if space in the Quality Assurance Building had been available? Probably not, given the amount of space it needed. But the experience had underscored the point: The park had no place to put new tenants.

However, a new player was about to enter the picture who could fill that need.

Where other men saw decay and ruin, David Shannon saw opportunity. Shannon was a born entrepreneur. While in his junior year studying economics and business at Wake Forest University, he and a fraternity brother started a business distributing solvents, degreasers, and other industrial chemicals. Upon graduation they set out to find warehouse space for their growing business, and ended up buying an old factory downtown. It was an ornate, three-story Victorian brick structure with bay windows and turrets, built by Nissen Wagon Works in 1893 during Winston-Salem's heady years of industrialization. The building had been vacant for years and the price was right.[12]

Once in, Shannon realized the building had the potential to house more than just his business. He rehabbed the unused space for offices and went looking for tenants. In short order he landed the N.C. Department of Human Services, which was looking for a regional office in Winston-Salem. Other tenants soon followed.

With this success, David Shannon found his true calling. Next he rehabbed an old building on North Trade Street for the local arts community, which was crying for cheap gallery and studio space; then the old Brown and Williamson tobacco factory on a kudzu-covered hill just north of downtown. By 1984 he had sold the chemical business and become a full-time developer.[13]

Although Shannon ventured into new construction, the rehabilitation of old buildings remained his passion. Inevitably, his thoughts turned to Reynolds' old tobacco factories downtown after Reynolds shuttered them, but his overtures to the company went nowhere. After Reynolds donated the factories to the county, Shannon resumed his efforts, but again he made no progress. County officials had space needs of their own and had commissioned a firm in Richmond to determine how to best use the buildings and land. Until that study was complete, they would not be entertaining any proposals.[14]

But as 1994 drew to a close, Shannon sensed that he might yet prevail. In all, the donated factories comprised more than one million square feet – far more than the county would need. The consultants had recommended that the county convert RJR factory No. 12, a five-story factory with 558,000 square feet, into offices and parking for county government and the Sheriff's Department. They recommended that Factory No. 265 be mothballed "until such time as improved market conditions dictate a feasible – hopefully private – redevelopment direction for the block bounded by First, Second, Chestnut and Patterson streets."[15]

No. 256 was really a complex of multiple buildings and connecting structures that dated back to the early years of R.J. Reynolds Tobacco Co. and was of sufficient significance to the rise of Reynolds – and concurrently of Winston-Salem – that it was on the study list for inclusion on the National Register of Historic Places. Here, Reynolds had built the first "modern" tobacco factory for the manufacture of plug chewing tobacco, with internal stairs and elevators, steam power, electric lights, and a sprinkler system to protect against fire, fed by two 6,000 gallon water tanks and pumps that could move 750 gallons a minute.[16]

Within the complex, 256-1 was the jewel. Built at the intersection of Second and Chestnut streets in 1891, it stood four stories high with an embellished brick exterior and modest pediment that immediately placed it in time compared with the more utilitarian architecture of 256-2 and 256-9, which were added later as separate buildings connected by tunnels and elevated corridors.[17] 256-9 occupied the corner of First and Chestnut streets, across First Street from the Quality Assurance building.

The consultant's report gave Shannon license to resume his discussions with county officials, but they were not about to turn the buildings over to any developer without a solid development plan. If Shannon wanted to get anywhere, he was going to have to have a concrete plan for converting the buildings – and commitments from some tenants to fill them. In short order, Shannon adjusted his vision for the buildings. Instead of filling the buildings with tenants who wanted to be near the research park, the building could be IN the research park.

Reynolds' historic Factory 256 complex. Developer David Shannon's desire to redevelop the historic factories coincided with the recommendation of park consultants to use Factory 256-9, at the far right, for speculative and incubator space.

Photo by David Rolfe, courtesy of Winston-Salem Journal

Unknown to him, Vernon George and the members of the Downtown Development Corp. had come to the same conclusion.

Meanwhile, the park management committee had plenty else to do. At the top of its list: assembling land for the park.

The ten acres identified for the park were split between five landowners. A key tract was held by Poindexter Lumber Co. along the north side of Business 40. Poindexter's land – 2.3 acres – accounted for almost a fourth of the park, and its highly visible position along the interstate dictated that it would play the key role of giving prospects their first impression of the park when they were being courted. Left unattended, what they would see would be stacks of lumber surrounding an oversized, aged metal shed and a small brick house that served as the company office.

The Fogle brothers had started the lumberyard in the 1880s, and through it had passed much of the wood that built Winston-Salem during its rise as a manufacturing powerhouse. Poindexter bought the business in 1970. The dingy lumberyard fit right in when the eastern flank of downtown was an industrial zone. But, even if it had not been situated in the core of the new park, it would stick out like a sore thumb and complicate the park's recruiting efforts.

Thomas Poindexter, the owner, was well aware of the plans for the research park, and that gave him leverage. The county tax office listed the property's value at $449,000, and an appraisal of Poindexter's property in September 1994 yielded a value of $520,000, but Poindexter was holding out for far more.[18] With no choice but to acquire the property, the Downtown Development Corp. was prepared to offer Poindexter a hefty premium for his land. Jerry Long, the former county commissioner and president of Reynolds Tobacco, had known Poindexter for a long time and approached him on behalf of the DDC. "He went by Took," Long said, "and I said, 'Took, you've got all this property tied up here and it's worth a certain appraised value. We're willing to pay you a million dollars. You can take this money and go out to Clemmons and build a new, modern facility. Otherwise you're forever going to be in competition with Lowe's and Home Depot.'"[19]

Poindexter declined. While Long continued to work on him, the DDC went about acquiring other tracts, especially the two-acre block of parking lots on the south side of First Street. The land was split between three different property owners.

R.J. Reynolds owned 1.25 acres of this block, along with two other tracts in the southeast corner of the park footprint. All three tracts had once served as parking lots for the employees working in No. 256, but their closure rendered the land surplus to Reynolds' needs and the company was a willing seller. Combined, they accounted for a quarter of the ten acres planned for the park. They appraised at a total value of $550,000. Reynolds agreed to sell them to the DDC for $595,700, and when the deal closed on Dec. 29, 1994, the first pieces of the puzzle were in place.[20]

Next came a small interior parking lot on the south side of First Street in the heart of the park. Gaither Jenkins, a prominent lawyer and former member of the City-County Planning Board, acquired the lot when Forsyth County bought it in order to trade it to Jenkins in exchange for a small tract he owned where the county wanted to build its new jail. The lot comprised 12,000 square feet – a little over a quarter of an acre – and had an appraised value of $81,000. Jenkins sold it for $90,000 on April 29, 1995.[21]

Another lot, sixth-tenths of an acre at the southeast corner of First and Church streets, held a parking lot and a small bail-bonding business owned by the heirs of Howard Hunt and man-

An aerial view of the area designated for the research park. The Quality Assurance Building is in the center. Poindexter Lumber Yard is at the far right.

Photo courtesy of the Forsyth County Public Library Photograph Collection

aged by Wachovia's trust division. It appraised at $252,000, but the owners held out for – and received – $310,000, an amount that when invested would yield interest equal to the annual income the property produced.[22]

Aside from assembling the land for the park, the committee's other big chore was to develop a master plan for the park. The DDC solicited requests for proposals at the start of 1994 and after a careful selection process, chose GBQC Architects of Philadelphia, in partnership with Brown and Keener Urban Design, to develop the master plan.

Their plan, delivered in January 1995, adhered closely to the vision offered by Hammer, Siler, George, with the notable exception that it identified Factory 256-9 as the best location for speculative and incubator space now that the old Quality Assurance building was out of the picture.[23] The notion was not GBQC's. Park advocates had suggested as much during their initial meetings with GBQC in June 1994. Jane Curry of GBQC readily agreed and provided the DDC with documents detailing how the firm created a shared incubator/start-up space for Penn State University.[24]

As the first phase of development, GBQC recommended creating an entrance boulevard into the park by expanding First Street, east of Church, into a four-lane street divided by a landscaped median. A quadrangle would be built at First and Chestnut streets, katty-corner from 256-9 and fronting on the Piedmont Triad Community Research Center. These steps, along with renovation of 256-9, "will create immediate evidence of the presence of the park; such an opportunity to make a dramatic first action is rare in research park development." Subsequent to this, four more buildings would be constructed: the first along Church Street, followed by three others on the south side of Belews Street on the land owned by Poindexter. A parking deck along Salem Avenue, between First and Belews streets, would complete the development.[25]

Overall, the plan envisioned an urban campus, integrated into downtown but sufficiently distinctive that it would constitute "a unique and identifiable place." Detailed guidelines were provided for landscaping, building design and materials, roof lines, streets, sidewalks, and parking lots. "The first mission of the park is to create a place for science, the second is to stimulate the economy of the region," the plan noted, adding with a bit of hyperbole, "The form of this plan creates the extraordinary opportunity for both to happen."[26]

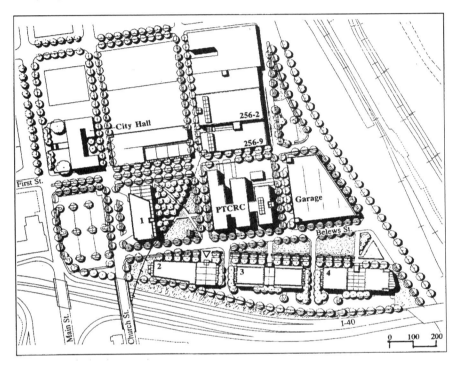

GBQC park development plan built upon the original plan sketch by HSG but added buildings (labeled 2, 3 and 4) on the Poindexter property.

To maintain the character of the park as it developed, GBQC outlined in broad strokes the provisions of protective covenants it suggested for the park. Creating these protective covenants, along with working through the myriad details required to turn the park into a reality, would consume the park management committee for the next year. There was a park logo to design, lighting standards to adopt and implement, a marketing plan to develop, and environmental assessments to complete of the proposed building sites. Until those buildings went up, the

DDC chose to continue to operate the parking lots it had acquired in order to bring in what income it could. This necessitated leases, insurance, and arranging for snow removal in the winter. Fiber-optic lines had to be extended into the park. Moving the Duke Power substation and assuring that the company could supply power for the new construction in the park consumed considerable effort.[27]

While all this proceeded, Jerry Long continued to work on Thomas Poindexter. They finally came to terms in the fall of 1995: Poindexter would sell his land in the park to the DDC for $1.1 million. When the sale closed on Jan. 31, 1996, the DDC finally had ownership of all the parcels in the park.[28] But as a condition of the sale, Poindexter required the DDC to also buy three-fourths of an acre that he owned outside the park footprint, on the south side of Business 40. The track held a warehouse with a railroad spur for lumber deliveries. It cost the DDC $200,000 more.[29]

Completion of the sale added more items to the park "to do" list: transferring the lease with a billboard company that had a billboard on Poindexter's land, arranging for asbestos removal from the buildings before the land was cleared, removing 440 feet of chain-link fence around the perimeter of the lumber yard, and contracting with a real estate agency to sell the warehouse on the south side of the interstate. The latter would prove to be a thorn in the DDC's side, once they learned that the warehouse was encroaching on the railroad right-of-way.[30]

But by far, the most time-consuming task involved drafting the protective covenants for the park. The document had to incorporate the correct balance of restrictions that would protect the park from diluting it into a mundane extension of downtown, while at the same time being flexible enough to accommodate a wide variety of potential tenants. Key to this would be the list of permitted uses, a task that generated a great deal of discussion. The committee finally settled on eight types of uses:

1. Laboratories and related facilities intended for basic and applied research development of medical or technology-

based products and services, or testing of medical or technology-based products and services.

2. Pilot plants in which prototype production processes can be tested and used for assembly of products of a medical or technological nature.

3. Corporate, regional and divisional headquarters of medical or technology-based or knowledge-driven companies and organizations.

4. Technology-dependent or computer-based facilities dedicated to the processing of data or analysis of information, provided these information services are supported by on-site research or product development.

5. Offices and related facilities of not-for-profit research or educational institutes as well as professional, training, research, scientific, medical or engineering associations.

6. Corporate and professional training facilities, provided that these facilities maintain ongoing cooperative relationships with universities in the Piedmont Triad region.

7. Services and retail uses incidental to, and in support of, any uses permitted in paragraphs (1) through (6) such as conference/hotel centers, restaurants, day care centers and banking and recreational facilities.

8. Any other facilities, including, but not limited to, residential dwelling units, reasonably related to the intended mission of the Research Park, provided that these uses are specifically approved by the board of the Piedmont Triad Research Park.

The last item was incorporated to help the research park stand out from its competitors, said Jack Steelman. "We had learned that most research parks were suburban in location and design. They were almost always 100 percent business. All the buildings were detached with no pedestrian connectivity and no opportunity for someone to live close to their research." Including a residential component in the research park would be one way it could stand out from its competitors.[31]

At the same time, the Downtown Development Corp. was actively working to restore residential living to the downtown mix. "We knew that for downtown Winston-Salem to evolve into the vibrant area we wanted it to be, there had to be full-time downtown residents," Steelman said. "That had been proven in city after city across the country." With its location on a corner, Reynolds Factory 256-9 gave the DDC just such an opportunity. Because it was a full floor taller than the adjoining 256-2, it was endowed with large windows on all four sides, making it perfectly suitable for loft condominiums.[32]

By the time the table of permitted uses was finalized, David Shannon was on board to redevelop 256-9. But it had not been an easy negotiation. Shannon was not interested in building condominiums in 256-9. He had a track record of success in converting old factories for business clients and had no experience in residential conversion. Furthermore, there was no precedent for factory lofts in Winston-Salem. It was an untested market, and Shannon did not want to be the guinea pig. However, he did – intensely – want to redevelop the old tobacco factories. Likewise, the DDC wanted him to have the job. Shannon had the requisite experience of working with older buildings, and a knack for filling them with tenants.[33]

With the DDC adamant about putting condos in 256-9, Shannon agreed – but only if he could limit his risk by getting the buildings at little or no cost. This was acceptable to the DDC. However, the county owned the buildings and the two entities would have to convince the county commissioners to approve their plan. Politically, the county commissioners could not simply hand over two blocks of prime downtown real estate to a private developer. Furthermore, the county was not about to turn loose the buildings without some assurance that they would, in fact, be redeveloped into a tax-generating asset.

The solution, worked out during discussions between the DDC, the county staff, and Shannon, was to effect a three-way transfer: The county would transfer the buildings to the DDC, and the DDC would make the buildings available to Shannon for the express purpose of converting them for use by the research park. But there were some catches: The county would not transfer the buildings until Shannon had pre-leased some space to a research park tenant. And the DDC was not about to give Shannon development rights without some sort of return for its asset.

Shannon addressed the DDC's conditions by agreeing to put 17 condominiums in 256-9 and giving the DDC a 10 percent interest in the redeveloped building. This left the issue of finding a tenant, which was no small hiccup, given that the research park was still largely a paper entity. There was little on the ground to show prospects other than the old Quality Assurance Building, an abandoned factory and some weed-strewn parking lots. Shannon, however, was confident in his ability to sell the vision. He'd been doing it for more than 10 years. And he knew that if he could just get that first tenant to commit on the promise of things to come, others would follow.[34]

Shannon found that tenant in Wiltek Medical, a medical-supplies company that Jon Wilson established in 1989 and was looking for space to grow. Given the park's work-in-progress status at the time, the move was not without risk. Presumably, Shannon structured the deal to make it a reasonable risk. But he also sold Wilson on the vision, as Wilson noted in the Winston-Salem Journal. "We are putting a lot on the line," he told a Journal reporter. But, he added that he believed the park would attract other high-tech companies.[35,36]

With all the details in place, the county commissioners unanimously approved a resolution on May 13, 1996, to transfer ownership of Factory 256 to the Downtown Development Corp., noting that the county would recover "the appraised value of the property which is $25,000 for the purposes of this resolution, within 10 years or less" from tax revenue generated by the rehabbed space.[37]

A month later, in a three-way closing, the county transferred the buildings to the DDC, which transferred them to the Piedmont Institute for Research and Technology, a new entity set up by Wolf Pond Development Corp. (Shannon) and the DDC to develop No. 256. The closing documents outlined the terms of their agreement: "Wolf Pond has expended certain funds and obtained one or more valuable leasehold commitments on behalf of the company (PIRT) and in furtherance of its business objectives. The parties acknowledge and agree that the deemed fair market value of these contributions made by Wolf Pond to or on behalf of the company is $112,500, in exchange for which Wolf Pond shall receive a 90 percent membership interest." In exchange for its 10 percent interest, the DDC contributed the property to the company. Concurrent with the closing, Central Carolina Bank provided a $983,242 loan for "construction and permanent financing for phase 1 of the rehabilitation and reuse" of RJR 256.[38]

With the transfer of the factories to a developer and the first tenants lined up, the Downtown Development Corp. and the research park management committee could rightly claim progress in the effort to turn the research park from a vision to a reality. But while the DDC had been absorbed with the minutia of developing the park, others involved in the technology movement could not help but sense that it was all taking too long. The momentum they had gained from the establishment of PTERC and the legislature's $3 million allocation had slowly dissipated. Their vision of using technology to re-make the local economy seemed to be stuck in low gear. Even the Wall Street Journal said so.

8   "WHEN THE GOING GETS TOUGH..."

If the community leaders striving to bring technology to Winston-Salem were ever tempted to indulge in despair, the spring of 1996 would have been the time. For eight years – eleven, from Doug Maynard's perspective – they had been working to lay the foundation for a new economy that, they hoped, would sustain Winston-Salem as the city's manufacturing titans succumbed to global trends beyond their control. Vernon George had validated their vision and given them an outline for creating a research park that was to be the engine for the transformation. And yes, the research park was slowly becoming a reality. But they had little else to show for their efforts.

The most flagrant symbol of their stymied efforts was the Piedmont Triad Engineering Research Center. PTERC, and the engineering expertise it would bring, was supposed to be the catalyst for change. Years of effort to bring engineering to Winston-Salem had finally paid off when the legislature authorized PTERC as part of the UNC system and gave it seed money. But the center was slowly atrophying. Among competing initiatives jostling for limited funds within the UNC system, PTERC was coming up short. No one was more aware of this than Pete Santago, who had used his graduate-school friendship with Harold Martin at NC A&T to foster the center that he now supervised.

After PTERC was up and running, Santago said, "a girl working over there (NC A&T) on her master's degree came over here. After that, we had a couple of other students from NC A&T, but we never had the drive and the impetus.... We had offices downtown in the old (Reynolds) R&D building and Ted Kaplan got us money (to get started).... But we never got any continuous funding and things didn't seem to pan out. We just couldn't get it going with the state."[1]

As if to rub salt on the wound, the Wall Street Journal had recently reported on a study that placed the Triad dead last when ranked by density of high-tech firms. Its February 14 edition reported that the economic research firm DRI/McGraw-Hill ranked the Triad lowest in density of high-tech firms among 114 metropolitan areas surveyed in the United States – lower even than Casper, Wyoming.[2]

The Wall Street Journal article was the proverbial wake-up call and the impetus for a meeting between Doug Maynard, Gayle Anderson and others promoting the technology agenda. It was time to step back and frankly assess where they stood, because, clearly, more needed to be done. This meeting was to be the start of a new initiative that would make the transformation to a technology-based economy a priority that would touch all facets of the community, from kindergartners on up.

They began by assessing their efforts thus far, and came to the conclusion – undeniable in light of the Journal story – that everything they had accomplished to date, as impressive as it was, could only be considered a "good start." Nonetheless, they noted, "significant gaps exist in the process for promoting technology and achieving economic development impact:

1. We do not have a comprehensive database regarding technology in our community.
2. We do not have a comprehensive and coordinated technology strategy.
3. We are not effectively organized to promote the growth of technology.

"There are elected chamber committees to pursue other major strategic goals such as industrial/business recruiting, film industry development and minority business development. There is also a public board to oversee tourism and convention recruiting. However, there is only a loosely organized volunteer group for technology. Likewise, the chamber has well-funded staff groups dedicated to convention and tourism (14 people,

$1.4 million) and industrial recruiting (three people, $175,000) but only part-time staff support for technology."[3]

The solution seemed obvious: The chamber should formally organize, elect, and fund a Technology Council, staffed by a chamber vice president, "to oversee efforts to develop the technology capabilities of Winston-Salem and Forsyth County and to ensure the development and growth of technology businesses."[4]

In coming up with this proposal, the committee had consulted with Walter Plosila, who had led just such a council in Maryland and who was now serving as executive director of the N.C. Alliance for Competitive Technologies. With Plosila's encouragement, the proposal envisioned a technology council that would have a broad mandate. In addition to developing a technology strategy, overseeing the research park, fostering technology transfer, and recruiting technology-based companies, the council would work to ensure that the city's infrastructure would support the growth of technology, and that its educational institutions "favor the growth of technology."[5]

The committee members spent some time refining their proposal and then pitched it to the chamber's board of directors, with the specific recommendation that the chamber again hire a consultant to guide the community through the process. If anyone had doubts about the merits of bringing in an outside consultant, the committee need only point to their experience with the research park. Before Vernon George made his study, they were hoping to build a clone of Research Triangle Park in the outlying farmland of Forsyth County. George brought the objective perspective and experience necessary to open their eyes to a new possibility. Likewise, the committee members noted, community leaders needed a professional and objective assessment of Winston-Salem's strengths, weaknesses, and opportunities if they were to efficiently, effectively, and quickly produce a blueprint for expanding the technology initiative to the community at large.[6] They also realized, human nature being what it is, that a plan developed by an outside consultant would inherently have more credibility than anything they might come up with on their own.

With the board's concurrence, the chamber staff sent out a request for proposals to consultants who might be capable of doing the job. In the meantime, the chamber began briefing community leaders on this next phase of their technology initiative. Essentially, the briefings served as a necessary forewarning to a broad swath of the city's leadership, given that the technology blueprint the chamber envisioned would require the cooperation of business, government, and educational institutions heretofore not involved. Properly executed, the push for technology could become THE overarching priority for the city at large.

The briefing started by recapping the work thus far and making it clear that more was needed to create a new economy based on technology: More partnerships between businesses and the city's universities, more high-tech industries, more research and development, more technology-savvy workers, and more venture capital. But it would take more than these obvious steps. The city needed to offer a lifestyle that could retain young, tech-savvy singles. It needed to streamline government regulations and permitting policies. It needed students to graduate from high school with a set of core technology skills that were more broadly applicable than the customized training offered for specific companies. And it needed "tech-friendly" spec space ready to serve the high-tech employers the community wanted to lure. The consultant would come up with a game plan for accomplishing all this and more.[7]

It was an ambitious plan, all the more so because no other city or county in the United States – and only a handful of states – had developed a technology blueprint,[8] and it captured the fancy of a man named Michael Alder. Alder initially had not been sent the RFP, but he had heard about it through the grapevine and requested a copy. "He had done the same thing for the state of Utah," Doug Maynard said. "He did a good job putting a tech blueprint in place for the governor. He was intrigued that a little city like Winston-Salem wanted to do this."[9]

Among those who responded to the RFP, the Technology Council selected six nationally recognized consulting teams for interviews, including Alder's ad-hoc group, whose members were not full-time consultants. In the late 1980s, the state of Utah had hand-picked this group of business managers, strategic planners, and marketing specialists from the private and public sectors and charged them with making Utah's economic dreams a reality. As a result of their work, Utah had more than doubled the number of technology companies in the state, growing from 850 firms in 1992 to 1,748 in 1996.[10]

In January 1997, Alder won the job and went to work. "We felt that we would not get a cookie-cutter approach," Maynard said. "He would not take a study he did for another city and change the names in his word processor. He didn't have anything to fall back on. He had to create this from scratch. And we liked him."[11]

While Alder assembled his team and began his study, the Downtown Development Corp. was focused on wrapping up the first phase of the Factory 256 conversion, which Shannon had renamed Albert Hall in honor of the Prince Albert pipe tobacco that Reynolds once produced in the building. As with any rehab project, conversion of 256-9 into Albert Hall carried its share of challenges, chief among them the need to gut the building of its industrial infrastructure. "There was so much stuff in there, a lot of equipment and a lot of duct work, a lot of electrical work and piping that was specific to the manufacturing process," Shannon said. "It was pretty heavy-duty stuff and was difficult to get out." The entire building was gutted down to the floors and concrete support columns and rebuilt with new interior walls, plumbing, electrical wiring, climate control, elevators, and windows.[12] The first three floors were allocated for commercial tenants; the fourth floor would be subdivided into 17 residential condominiums. Total cost of the renovation would come to $2.7 million.[13]

With conversion of 256-9 underway, the Downtown Development Corp. soon realized that a committee meeting sporadically could not adequately oversee the project and park operations. In September 1996 it adopted an operating plan as part of a memorandum of understanding between the DDC, the chamber, the city of Winston-Salem, and Winston-Salem Business Inc. that designed Jack Steelman of the city's Development Office as the chief staff person for the park, assisted by Shelly Treadwell of the chamber. Winston-Salem Business Inc. would assume chief responsibility for marketing the park.[14]

The memorandum assigned Steelman an ambitious "to-do" list for the coming year that showed just how much work remained to be done. It included completing improvements to the old Duke Power parking lot and building a new parking lot on the old Poindexter property, extending First Street to Salem Avenue, participating in the design and development of the park "campus quadrangle," working with a developer to get a spec building under construction, marketing the remaining space in Albert Hall, coordinating overall park marketing with Winston-Salem Business Inc., and sprucing up the park in time for the chamber's first-ever "Connectivity" exposition.[15]

The latter was an event the chamber initiated in order to do something proactive to shake the technology initiative out of its doldrums while Michael Alder worked on the technology blueprint. The concept was simple: Connect potential investors with the researchers at the medical school who were developing promising new technologies. As an added benefit, the exposition would bring added exposure to the research park

Albert Hall, shortly after its grand opening.
Photo courtesy of Winston-Salem Journal

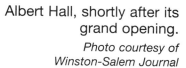

and hopefully, bring some leads for new tenants.[16]

By late December sufficient progress had been made on Albert Hall for Wiltek to move in. The company took the entire third floor, giving it 25,000 square feet for its 40 employees and the 20 more it planned to hire over the coming year. In February it was joined by another medical company, Salem Products LLC, and a photography studio, Black Horse Studio. (Black Horse qualified for tenancy as an "imaging" company.)[17] Other tenants soon followed: Marathon Group in April, PharmaSTAT in May 1997 and Orthofix in July. With the exception of Orthofix, all were small start-ups that leased modest amounts of space. Nonetheless, the grand opening of the building, held April 24, 1997, was cause for celebration and more tangible proof that the vision of a downtown research park was becoming a tangible reality.[18]

However, it was going to take a lot of money to finish the job. Even as dignitaries gathered to celebrate the opening of Albert Hall, Steelman was preparing an updated cost estimate for completing the master plan for the park at the request of the Downtown Development Corp. board. In a memo to the board, he reported, "There are $9,319,000 worth of needs remaining and we have a current balance of some $260,000 from the state grant." On the positive side, Steelman noted that actual costs were running under estimates. "It will also be of value to note that nearly six million of the nine needed is for a parking deck at the end of the project, which, hopefully, would be developed by the city as have other downtown public parking decks." The $9.3 million included $516,000 for the campus quadrangle, $886,000 for underground utilities, $290,000 to relocate Belews Street, $200,000 for opening Second Street into the park, $616,000 for a small park fronting the proposed buildings south of Belews Street, $510,000 for interim parking lots, $5.84 million for the parking deck, and $461,000 for streetscape improvements, signs, curb and gutter, and other pedestrian enhancements.[19]

The quadrangle was to be the focal point of the park. As envisioned in the master plan, it would be about the size of the town square in Old Salem and would be key to giving the park its "research campus" atmosphere. But the west side of the quadrangle was to be defined by the first new building planned for the park, and plans for it were dragging along.

After a months-long process of soliciting proposals from qualified developers, the Downtown Development Corp. had selected Fowler Jones Beers Construction Co. of Winston-Salem to build "Research One," as the committee was referring to the building. FJB brought an impressive resumé to the project. Since 1980 it had completed 69 laboratory projects worth a total of $871 million in Texas, Florida, Georgia, Virginia, Tennessee, and North Carolina. These projects had given it working relationships with some of the biggest names in the pharmaceutical industry, among them Bayer Consumer Care, Ciba-Geigy, Hoffman LaRoche Inc., Merck & Co., Pfizer Consumer Health Care Group, Whitehall-Robbins, and Wyeth. The company was also a known entity to the city, having built such projects as the Benton Convention Center, the annex to the Lawrence Joel Veterans Memorial Coliseum, the performance lab at the NC School of the Arts, and the student union at Winston-Salem State University.[20]

This experience was more than adequate to prove that it had the ability, experience, and financial backing to design and construct an 80,000-square-foot speculative building that could accommodate either office or research use. In choosing FJB, DDC members hoped that the developer's extensive network of relationships with research and pharmaceutical companies would bring new tenants to the research park. But as a back-up plan, city officials said they were prepared to occupy up to half of the space in the new building. The city staff had long outgrown the space available in City Hall, leaving half a dozen city departments scattered around the downtown in leased space. City officials had long wanted to consolidate them into one location near City Hall, and Research One could fit the bill nicely. Accordingly, the DDC added to its project requirements the provision that the spec space be able to accommodate city offices at a reasonable price, and that it be suitable for rehab into research space should the city move out.[21]

During July 1996, the DDC and Fowler Jones Beers negotiated

the terms for a development agreement that called for the contractor to begin construction of Research One "if either of the following conditions have been met: FJB has obtained lease commitments from research companies equal to one-half of the usable square feet in the building, or the city or the City-County Utilities Commission has committed to purchase one half of the usable square feet in the building.... Should the city commit to purchase one half of the building, it is expressly understood by the parties that FJB will construct at least 40,000 square feet of additional speculative research space with or without having any other leases in place."[22]

With the agreement drafted and FJB's track record, DDC members were justifiably optimistic that the Research Park was poised to shed its image as a collection of RJR cast-offs. The brochure FJB produced to market the building made it easy to visualize: The expanse of cracked asphalt parking lots along Church Street would give way to a handsome three-story brick building that borrowed many design cues from City Hall a block away, notably the window headers and balustrade across the top.

But a new controversy immediately marred the vision. In working out the details of the development agreement, FJB wanted to amend the provisions such that it would begin construction only if one of three conditions was met: Either: (1) Research tenants committed to leasing half the space in the building; (2) If the city bought half the building, half of remaining space was pre-leased; or (3) If the city leased half the building, a quarter of remaining space was pre-leased.[23]

Allen Joines, the city's development director, was the DDC's point man in the negotiations. In a memo to the DDC executive committee, Joines noted that the second and third conditions "are contrary to the understanding we all had relative to the FJB commitment to the project. Therefore, it is my feeling that if FJB holds firm with (these) conditions, that we, in fact, have a breach of the conditions under which they were chosen." Further complicating the issue, Joines noted, was news that the NationsBank building downtown, which housed several city departments, might soon be sold, raising the possibility that the city might need to vacate the building within five years. "Given this scenario, it may be more cost-effective for the city to plan a permanent space location, rather than participating in the interim research park building."[24]

Chamber President Fred Nordenholz had a measured response, noting that the second and third conditions would be moot if the city had to go elsewhere. "I still favor going with FJB. My original decision was based on the marketing clout they have as a world-wide company (and the commitment Alan Jones made to use that clout). Their marketing capability is superior to the other contenders and that has not changed."[25]

The DDC chose to accept FJB's terms, as reflected in one of the tasks included in Jack Steelman's work plan: "Complete feasibility study of Research I building by Fowler Jones Beers with the goal of commencing construction by January 1997." As it would turn out, the building would not be under construction by January 1. Nor would be it under construction when the park celebrated the grand opening of Albert Hall in April 1997, nor by December 1997 when Michael Alder turned in his long-awaited technology blueprint.

The chamber's expectation that Alder would not give the city a cookie-cutter action plan proved to be well-founded. Alder and his team of experts burrowed deep into the city's economic infrastructure before drafting their blueprint. The document they presented in December 1997 was a true blueprint in every figurative sense of the word, providing both a series of overall strategies that constituted the "big picture" of how to hasten the development of a technology sector in the local economy, and detailed recommendations on how to implement each strategy.

The blueprint recommended six strategies:

1. Exploit for the long term the city's greatest technology asset, the medical school at Wake Forest, and in the near term emphasize high-tech manufacturing (such as Tobaccoville) and new media technologies at the NCSA film school.

2. Enlist Wachovia Bank and BB&T to assist with capital

formation and development of new financial products and services that would attract and build a high-tech community.

3. Build the infrastructure necessary to attract and retain technology-based businesses.
4. Exploit Forsyth County's excellent quality of life while building an environment to foster high-tech start-ups.
5. Encourage the city's wealthy, business-savvy citizens to lend their business mentoring skills and invest their financial resources.
6. Commit to this goal for the long term by educating community residents in "the literacy of technology."

The plan also identified two long-known shortcomings that needed to be addressed: the lack of seed and venture capital to assist promising high-tech start-ups, and the lack of graduate engineering education in the community. Given that Doug Maynard and Pete Santago had spent more than a decade trying to rectify the latter issue without great success, it was no doubt disheartening to see it in print, even though they themselves had acknowledged this shortcoming in their discussions with Alder.[26]

The blueprint made clear that the medical school would have to be the engine for the city's

Michael Alder sought out the city's RFP for developing a technology master plan because he was intrigued by the thought of a city trying to remake its economy.

Photo courtesy of Mike Alder

technology economy, with the other recommendations playing a supporting role, and it noted that the school "has indicated a strong desire" to accept this responsibility. "That commitment from the university is crucial to long-term development of a technology transfer/commercialization system that otherwise may not be possible. It is essential that the community reciprocates and assists in every way possible to help build the university." The medical school "needs to be given 'most favored status' in the community to achieve its growth potential. Public meetings should constantly be focused on the school's needs and how the community can help."[27]

To jump-start the plan, Alder identified several research areas that might be exploited as new business opportunities, among them, non-invasive imaging of the gastro-intestinal tract; using the discovery of a renal bile acid transporter to develop new drugs for controlling cardiovascular disease, cholesterol and Crohn's disease; using viral M proteins to kill cancer cells or viral-infected cells; and developing commercial applications of patented molecules licensed from the medical school.[28]

But the blueprint alone would not be sufficient to transform the economy, Alder warned. "To accomplish these objectives will require a new organization that will coordinate the programs and initiatives necessary to change the present environment in Winston-Salem." This organization, Alder said, should be an umbrella group that would oversee the multiple technology initiatives and would have enough clout to make things happen.

For purposes of the report, Alder called this putative organization the Winston-Salem Technology Venture Authority (WSTVA). Under it would be seven subsidiary organizations "necessary to the success of the total technology development initiative." These Alder identified as:

1. The Piedmont Triad Research Park, which Alder recommended be placed under the authority but have a separate director and staff;

2. The Winston-Salem Technology Innovation Center, a university-operated entity to assist start-up technology-

based businesses;

3. A university business assistance office, to assist with grant writing and formation of cooperative research agreements;
4. A technology development and commercialization fund to finance patents and market studies for new companies before they have raised initial capital;
5. Forsyth Angel Investors, a group of independently wealthy individuals willing to invest in promising new ventures and to mentor new enterprises through their early stages of growth;
6. The Technology Venture Capital Fund, a new city-based venture capital fund, ideally anchored by local banks with assistance from the state and individual investors, that would demonstrate the citywide commitment to technology development; and
7. The North Carolina Center for New Business Creation, a new entity that would oversee the operations of the technology development and commercialization fund and the Technology Innovation Center.

"To successfully start and build these new pieces of infrastructure and to raise the necessary capital for investment activities will require strong support from the leaders and citizens of the county," Alder warned. "The newly proposed infrastructure will require substantial support from volunteers for fund-raising, mentoring, legal assistance, accounting assistance, etc."[29]

Overseeing the overall effort would be a WSTVA board comprising the city's ranking business and community leaders. "The WSTVA board will raise funds and act as fiduciary over the funds needed to operate the recommended new infrastructure. This organization will plan and coordinate all the programs and activities necessary to the success of the total technology development initiative. The WSTVA will also be responsible for recruiting and using volunteers to perform many important blueprint tasks." Crucially, "The new authority should be led by a visionary and respected community leader." A volunteer board, however, was not sufficient. "WSTVA will need to employ a dynamic president who can oversee its programs and operations while developing its vision of the future."[30]

As to a "visionary and respected community leader" to chair the new board, there was immediate consensus among the membership of the Technology Council: Wake Forest University President Tom Hearn. Hearn had supported all of Doug Maynard's efforts dating back to the late 1980s, including the initiatives to connect the medical school to the state microwave network and to start the Piedmont Triad Engineering Research Center. "We wanted someone who the whole community respected and had an interest in (technology)," Maynard said. "Tom had been active in the United Way and had been active in starting Leadership Winston-Salem. So Tom had the interest in Winston-Salem and we felt if we could get him to chair it, we would have no difficulty getting other players to join." Hearn readily agreed. "Tom didn't take long to make decisions," Maynard said. "We didn't have to twist his arm or anything.[31]

The question was, would the rest of Winston-Salem's leadership be equally ready to buy into a broader vision for transforming the local economy? Although Hearn had agreed to chair the new technology board, it would not have the requisite horsepower to accomplish the desired transformation if it did not include the city's top civic and business leaders.

This crucial question would be answered on Jan. 5, 1998, when the chamber's Technology Council unveiled Alder's report at a high-level community meeting in the auditorium at the Southeastern Center for Contemporary Art. "Up to this point it had just been a few of us in the chamber," Maynard said. "This was really going to be the moment of truth that would determine if we could get the wider city leadership to make this a community-wide effort."[32]

Before a packed house, Chamber Chairman Jerry Long opened the meeting with a few words of introduction and ceded the podium to Maynard, who recapped the efforts to date and explained the chamber's vision for the future; why a technology blueprint was needed; and why the chamber selected Alder's team. Alder discussed the highlights of his blueprint, and then Maynard played the trump card for the meeting: "When we were discussing the ideal individual to chair this newly created technology initiative," he told the assembled dignitaries, "Tom Hearn was the unanimous choice.... Since Wake Forest University's involvement must be extensive to ensure the success of this effort, I am pleased to announce that he has accepted that role." Hearn then said a few words, effectively sealing the deal when it came time to ask people to serve on the board.[33]

"It wasn't a difficult pitch," Maynard said. "Everyone at the time was concerned about the economy and what we needed to do.... People saw that it was a good thing. But I went on Tom's behalf, which made it a lot easier. Everybody we asked agreed to do it."[34]

The board was a veritable who's who of the senior business and academic leadership in Winston-Salem. Bud Baker, the CEO of Wachovia Corp., and Andy Schindler, the CEO of Reynolds Tobacco, served as vice-chairmen. Members included the heads of BB&T, Sara Lee Knit Products, Flow Automotive, Wachovia Bank of North Carolina, Baptist Hospital, Novant Health, the NC School of the Arts, Winston-Salem State University, Salem College, Forsyth Technical Community College, and the Wake Forest Medical School; representatives of the city's two largest law firms; and the chairmen of the Chamber of Commerce, the Downtown Development Corp., and Winston-Salem Business Inc. Doug Maynard served as an ex-officio member, as did Congressman Richard Burr, prudently named to the board to champion any projects that might benefit from federal support. In all, the board numbered 40 people.[35] Hearn formed an executive committee of twelve to deal with most issues in a timely manner.[36]

The first board meeting was called for March 31, 1998. As with any such high-powered board, much of the heavy lifting was done by others working behind the scenes. During the weeks leading up to the meeting, a Community Technology Initiative Planning Committee led by Doug Maynard began thinking through the specifics of how the new board would operate in order to present concrete proposals for the board to consider at its first meeting.[37] The committee split up into working groups to take the most pressing issues: organizational structure, financial planning, venture capital, and the business creation center. None of the committee members much cared for Alder's proposed name (Winston-Salem Technology Venture Authority), they wanted something more dynamic and less bureaucratic; preferably a name that did not include the words "authority" or "foundation." The committee members also made plans to see what they could learn through visits to other cities, such as Birmingham and Richmond, that had similar organizations.[38]

In the end the committee recommended that the new group identify itself as the "North Carolina Emerging Technology Alliance" and that it adopt a much more "lean" structure than that recommended by Alder: The alliance itself would not have a staff but exist as a volunteer entity to oversee a limited liability corporation with a paid staff responsible for the research park, a technology business incubator, the center for business creation, and WinstonNet. Venture capital initiatives would be led separately by John McKinnon, a former president of Sara Lee Corp. and retired dean of Wake Forest's Babcock School of Management.[39]

While this committee was hammering out the details for the NCETA board, Wake Forest was already moving ahead with a crucial element of the plan. In mid-December 1997, an ad hoc University Task Force on Technology Transfer and Business Development delivered a half-inch thick report laying out a route "to maximize collaboration between the Winston-Salem business community and the university."[40]

John Anderson, Wake Forest's vice president for finance and administration, empaneled the task force specifically to review the Alder blueprint and recommend a way to fulfill its recommendation that the university become the "technological development engine" for the city. "By combining resources with the city, the university has the opportunity to leverage its own research investment with community funds for business development. Should the companies produced by this partnership succeed, they will produce significant income for the university." Maynard and Jay Moscowitz, the associate dean for research development, served as co-chairs of the task force.[41]

The past seven years had given university leaders a taste of what they stood to gain with the plan. In 1991, faculty members had reported seven inventions to Wake Forest's Technology Transfer Service and filed three patent applications. The school received no royalty income that year. Over the next few years, awareness of the community's interest in developing technology grew among researchers, and in increasing numbers they began stepping forward with their ideas. By the 1996-1997 school year, the service reported 132 invention disclosures, 103 patent applications, and royalty income of $613,900. And yet, only one full-time employee at the university worked on technology transfer. To fully leverage the intellectual property generated by research at the school, a broad-ranging program was needed to move promising research out of the lab and into the marketplace.[42]

To accomplish this, the task force recommended four initiatives:

1. Adapting the Alder Blueprint (which was in draft form at the time) to create an entity similar in function to Alder's proposed Technology Venture Authority, only with a simpler structure to make it less bureaucratic and easier for researchers to deal with. As an alternative, the university could create its own organization parallel to the authority, but this would be a costly duplication of effort, and carried the risk that the community might perceive this as a university initiative and not meriting broad community support.

2. Starting a formalized, ongoing strategic planning process comprising both the medical school and the university to identify the most promising research areas and recruiting, if necessary, key scientists with expertise that would complement these research areas.

3. Creating an in-house fund to finance applied research into embryonic discoveries that require more development before they can attract venture capital. Federal grants from the National Institutes of Health and the

National Science Foundation supported only basic research, but not applied development to demonstrate a discovery's commercial potential to investors.

4. Expanding the university's Technology Transfer Service into an Office of Technology Transfer and Business Development and staffing it with six full-time employees.[43]

With Maynard, Moscowitz, and Anderson involved with both the task force and the chamber's Community Technology Initiative Planning Committee, the task force's rationale for simplifying Alder's proposed infrastructure gained currency among members of the latter committee and became part of the agenda for the first meeting of the NCETA board.

During a two-hour working lunch at the Bridger Field House at Groves Stadium, Maynard briefed the board on the Blueprint for Technology, followed by Moscowitz, who presented the university's Technology Transfer and Business Development Plan. To illustrate the potential of technology development, two scientists at the school presented their research. Dr. David Vining presented his work on virtual endoscopy, a technology that would be ready for commercialization in two to three years; and Dr. Si Yi Chen presented his research on a genetic approach to cancer treatment, which was an early-stage discovery that would require applied research to verify and develop its commercial potential. Next John Anderson and John Boehme described the WinstonNet initiative, a plan to use excess capacity in the fiber connection between the two Wake Forest campuses to connect all the community's major institutions.[44]

Following these briefings, the board got down to business. The working group presented its recommendations and one by one, the board accepted the proposed name (N.C. Emerging Technology Alliance), organization, legal structure, and budget. It formed a search committee to develop a job description and hire a national search firm to assist in hiring a chief executive officer for the corporate entity that would run the research park and coordinate the other technology initiatives. The minutes of that meeting succinctly noted that the meeting concluded "with the board accepting the challenges of this new community venture." Henceforth, the executive committee would attend to the details.[45]

Two years had passed in the quest to make technology transformation a citywide priority. The technology advocates now had a roadmap and the backing of the city's collective leadership – or so they thought. Events would prove soon enough that the battle was only half won.

9   GETTING SERIOUS

Bill Dean vividly remembers the first meeting of what would become the Winston-Salem Alliance. Dean had been in town for less than a year, having been recruited from Huntsville, Alabama, to be CEO of the Piedmont Triad Research Park, when he was invited to a meeting called by L.M. "Bud" Baker, the CEO of Wachovia Corp.

The movement to reverse downtown Winston-Salem's years of decline was gathering momentum. Baker intended to put Wachovia four-square behind the effort and had called a meeting to get the rest of the downtown leadership on board. Baker's vision was ambitious and practical: He was not about to create another advocacy group. He wanted this group to have the power to make things happen – and that meant money, lots of it. Ultimately, he would persuade and cajole the deep pockets in town to join Wachovia in creating a $40 million pool of money, privately controlled, to do what they deemed necessary.

But this was still months away when Baker assembled the leaders of Winston-Salem's leading corporations and institutions in Wachovia's board room high in the new Wachovia skyscraper on Second Street. Bill Dean, as CEO of the research park, was among those present. "So they take a white board and they say, 'Let's start listing the most important things that will help with the downtown area.' I'm thinking, This is good. With the talk when I was being recruited, the park has to be right up there as one of the things to help the downtown grow."[1]

Dean chose not to say anything, partly because he was a newcomer to the community, and partly to see where the research park stood in the eyes of the community leadership. And he watched in dismay as one idea and another was thrown out with nary a word about the research park. Eventually, it was mentioned, almost as an afterthought. "Once I saw that we were number nineteen I saw my work was cut out for me. I immediately called Tom Hearn. 'Tom, we have a problem.' He laughed about it. He said, 'There's a lot of thoughts and a lot of ideas.'" Dean's view, naturally, was less nonchalant, given his decision to leave the best job he had ever had when he accepted the offer to come to Winston-Salem.[2]

He was a banker by training, a Southerner born and raised in Mississippi who had spent all his adult life in Alabama. Dean's career took him to Huntsville, where the Cummings Research Park was starting to come into its own. As the regional CEO for Colonial Bank Group, Dean was constantly engaged in the park's activities, both as a financier for promising tech start-ups and as a member of a number of boards of directors for companies in the park. And when Dean determined that he was ready for a new career path, the community asked him to take over as manager of the park. "I thought I would take the job in Huntsville for a short period of time," Dean said. "I planned to go back into the financial industry in some capacity.[3]

"But I got engaged in what was going on in the research park. I found it very interesting to learn about the many changes coming about in space and science and electronics, and it had a big business component." He stayed, and during his tenure the research park grew into the second largest in the world, with 95 buildings totaling seven million square feet on 3,800 acres. More than 22,000 people were employed by 170 companies in the park, among them McDonnell Douglas, TRW, General Electric, Hewlett Packard, and Rockwell International.[4]

Given the success of Cummings, Dean was often the subject of recruiting pitches from research parks looking for new leadership. He declined them all, even the offer to lead a research park started by a large and prestigious university in the Northeast. "I'm a Southern boy, and culturally, I didn't fit that market.... After visiting there numerous times, my wife and I decided to stay in Huntsville. I promise you, you could not blow me out of Huntsville. It was a dynamic community. And then I got this phone call."[5]

It was the executive recruiting firm that NCETA had retained to find a park director, and this time, Dean was going to accept. "When they said Wake Forest and Winston-Salem, I laughed. I said, 'I know Tom Hearn.' Number one, Tom's from Alabama, and number two, Tom and my wife are first cousins. I said, 'I want to talk to Tom and see what the opportunity is.' So we called Tom and he was very candid with me about the situation in the community and what had transpired, and he asked about my level of interest. I said, 'If it's what you say it is, I have a high level of interest.'

Bill Dean arrived from Cummings Research Park looking for a new challenge – and found it.

Photo by Megan Morr, courtesy of Winston-Salem Journal

But I was concerned that he was president of the university and he and my wife are first cousins, so he had to remove himself" from the hiring process.[6]

"I was running a park that is a well-oiled machine. And knowing in the back of my mind that I had been doing mergers and acquisitions, I was ready for a different challenge. I thought that I could transfer this knowledge and experience, based on my understanding of the needs of the research park, to get it developed."

But, as he realized a year after he arrived, Dean had made an unwarranted assumption. "I had a great understanding of North Carolina's technology development, having studied and watched Research Triangle Park like you watch your big brother.

I carried that over to this community. I made the assumption that the same enthusiasm, the same knowledge and under-standing of how (RTP) took place, was here as well.

"It was contrary to the fact. It was two different cultures, two different areas." Winston-Salem was built on manufacturing. In comparison, research parks can seem to develop at a glacial pace. "You have to have the infrastructure and an environment in place that is conducive to attracting (the sort of companies) that RTP attracts. RTP didn't do that overnight. But if you don't have an understanding of this, you want it to be today."[7]

By the time Dean accepted the offer to lead the research park in March 1999, an eventful year had passed since the NCETA board agreed that the park needed a full-time executive.

Financially, NCETA was in good shape, thanks to the efforts of Walter McDowell of Wachovia. Through his efforts, NCETA finished the year with pledges totaling more than $1.2 million to sustain the organization for its first five years. John McKinnon had commitments for $6 million of the $10 million goal for the early start-up venture fund.[8] Even more promising was the prospect that the stalled development efforts were finally regaining some momentum.

The initial effort with Fowler Jones Beers to put up a spec building had never come to fruition, for lack of sufficient pre-leasing to trigger construction. But in the late spring of 1998, a new opportunity arose out of the blue that held the prospect of jump-starting the process. It came courtesy of Don Angell, a flamboyant businessman and developer who brought NCETA the proverbial offer that it could not refuse.

Angell was a born entrepreneur who, at the age of 27, ditched his training as a mortician to start a nursing home. Out of that seed he built a business that operated 10,000 beds in 14 states. Along the way he began developing retirement commu-nities and hotels. Angell had a knack for sensing opportunities where others saw none, and he sensed one in the southeast cor-ner of downtown. The two main hotels for serving downtown were five blocks from the headquarters of Wachovia and BB&T. And there were no accommodations to serve the new research park. Angell figured that a hotel serving those two employment centers could do well. And the city just happened to own some land right where such a hotel might best be located.

In short order Angell made an appointment with Steelman and Allen Joines, who had been promoted to assistant city manager overseeing economic development, to inquire about buying the land. It was not the first time a developer had approached the city with plans for the land. Initially, Angel was met with the same response the others had received. "Allen told him we couldn't sell it because that's where our employees parked," Steelman said. "In response Don said, so, he needed a site for a hotel and the city needed a parking deck. Was there anything else? Allen said, 'Yeah, that's also where we were planning one day to build our own office building to consolidate all the (city) departments that are scattered around downtown.' And Don said, 'Well, OK. I'll build a hotel, a parking deck, and an office building.'"[9]

At the NCETA executive committee meeting on June 22, 1998, Joines optimistically reported on his discussions with Angell, and the opportunity that construction of a parking deck presented to leverage development of the spec building the park needed. Joines noted that the spec building could be financed by a consortium of bank loans. Alternatively, he said, Wachovia could invest in the building and agree to occupy half of it in order to secure construction financing. The other half would be built as shell wet lab space. The committee directed Joines to study the latter option.[10]

Meanwhile, David Shannon was steadily making progress with the old RJR 256 complex.

By June 1998, Albert Hall, the old 256-9 building, was completed and all but filled. The list of tenants now included NetUnlimited, a provider of computer network and Internet services that was attracted to the research park by both its infrastructure and its atmosphere, said Jim Capps, one of the investors in the company. "For our business, running a data center, some of the most important things are where the fiber is, and clean, reliable power. They had lit the area up pretty well with fiber, and it was right next to a (Duke Power) substation.

"The park was also attractive to us because of the opportunity to be in a place with a lot of other small, growing companies. We could use their services, they could use our services. Plus the rates were very competitive, and it was high-quality space: high ceilings, wood floors, the columns – it was beautiful space. We really believed in what Gayle Anderson and all of them were trying to do in the park and we wanted to help foster that."[11]

Progress on 256-2 was coming along nicely. The lofts in Albert Hall had proven so popular that Shannon was building 20 more condos in 256-2. More importantly, he had secured an anchor tenant for the building, Frisby Technologies. The company made high-tech insulating and cooling foams and thermal additives. Shannon began courting owner Greg Frisby in the fall of 1996 when he attended the chamber's Connectivity Expo and shared his desire to consolidate his company operations, which were split between New York and South Carolina.[12]

The end result was Frisby's agreement to lease 25,000 square feet in the renovated factory to house the company's headquarters, research and development, product testing, warehousing, prototype development, and assembly operations. Frisby also took an option for another 25,000 square feet, and in return, the building was to be known as the Frisby Technology Center.[13]

Conversion of the building was on schedule for a late September opening when Jack Steelman and Allen Joines sat in on a meeting of the mayors of all the municipalities in Forsyth County, being held in City Hall. It was Aug. 27, 1998. During the meeting Bill Stuart, the unflappable city manager, stuck his head in the door and calmly motioned for Steelman to step outside the room. He led Steelman to a window. Smoke was rising the next block over. "Jack," Stuart said, "your project is on fire. You might want to get over there."[14]

Fire investigators later learned that demolition workers using welding torches accidently started the fire. The day before, they had been removing a cooling tower from the factory complex when a spark from a torch lit a pile of debris and heavily varnished redwood on the ground next to the rear of

256-2. The workmen tried to stomp out the fire, then doused it with water from a garden hose. When they left that night, they thought the fire was out.[15] But the incident made a lasting impression on Jon Wilson of Wiltek, who observed the episode. If those guys aren't more careful, he thought to himself, they're

Photo by Allen Aycock, courtesy of Winston-Salem Journal

Photo courtesy of the Forsyth County Public Library Photograph Collection

A stray spark from a welding torch destroyed all but one section of RJR's historic Factory 256 complex just days before its renovations were completed.

going to set the building on fire.[16]

In fact, they already had. When the workmen returned the next day, they noticed that the debris pile was smoldering. They tried to kill the embers by scattering the pile. But this gave the embers sufficient oxygen to re-ignite the flames, thanks to the brisk wind whipping through downtown as Hurricane Bonnie approached the North Carolina coast. Afterwards, an office worker in Albert Hall would tell of seeing the workmen pouring buckets of water on the flames in an attempt to put them out. But it was too late. Year upon year of built-up varnish on the wood provided an accelerant that was impervious to water. The fire grew and at 10:36 a.m., the workers called the Fire Department.[17]

The first fire engine arrived at 10:40, followed by a second truck a minute later, and a ladder truck the minute after that. But it was already too late. 256-2 was rapidly becoming engulfed in flame, fed by the building's bone-dry wooden floors and columns. Inside, carpet, debris, tanks of oxygen for the welding torches, and wood stacked inside for renovations provided yet more fuel for the fire. Even as the flames spread, more fire stations were responding. Within 23 minutes, the Fire Department had five pumpers and four ladder trucks on the scene, but they were making no progress. Wind gusts of more than 20 miles an hour were whipping the flames into a frenzy, threatening to set fire to the adjacent buildings, including Albert Hall. Firefighters made a sweep through the building in case anyone was still foolish enough to be inside.[18]

David Shannon watched the initial firefighting efforts with mounting despair. The conversion of 256 was not only a significant business investment, but the climax of his professional career. In his estimation, no other old building in Winston-Salem could match its historic significance. Here, Reynolds had developed and produced the revolutionary Camel cigarette that brought Reynolds unprecedented wealth and spurred the city's development as a manufacturing powerhouse. But for Factory 256, Winston-Salem as he knew it would not exist. Shannon returned to his office, unable to bear the sight.[19]

Downtown, in the Piedmont Club on the 19th floor of the

BB&T Building, Phil Johnston, the chief executive of Pilot Therapeutics, was meeting with his board of directors, going over the final preparations for opening the company's new headquarters in the Frisby Technology Center. One director noticed the smoke in the sky. Soon they all were at the window, where, far below, they could see their new offices going up in flames. Dumbfounded, all they could say was, "That's us."[20]

Jim Capps of NetUnlimited had spent the morning in Greensboro and saw the smoke in the distance as he got on Interstate 40 for the trip back to Winston-Salem. His sense of foreboding grew with each passing mile as it became clear that the fire was downtown. Then he reached the bridge over U.S. 52, affording a clear view of the research park. His worst fears were realized.[21]

While some firefighters attacked the blaze, others trained a steady flow of water on Albert Hall in an attempt to keep it from catching fire. Still more were dousing an elevated breezeway connecting 256-2 with the southernmost portions of 256-1 to the north. And still the fire grew. A block away, administrators in the Forsyth County Jail evacuated the 732 inmates to the Joel Coliseum annex. The 120 employees working in the Piedmont Triad Community Research Center were also evacuated. By now, 170 firemen were battling the fire with 13 pumpers and five ladder trucks. By 1:30 p.m. 256-2 was starting to collapse, and the firemen were now battling flames that had taken hold on the roof of 256-1. Fire Chief John Gist began to worry that it might next spread to RJR Factory No. 12, the next building to the north.

The firefighters were facing a truly apocalyptic blaze. Temperatures inside the burning factories were reaching 1,500 degrees Fahrenheit. Firefighters were succumbing to heat exhaustion within 10 minutes. The heat was so intense that it was too dangerous to put firefighters on the ladder trucks; the nozzles at the top of the ladders were remotely operated. Even still, the heat burned the wiring on the ladders. Wind-borne sparks from the blaze jumped south of Business 40 and started grass fires in Old Salem. All of the 256 complex, save Albert Hall, was a roaring inferno. The fire burned for eight hours.[22]

It was a great irony that fire destroyed the 256 factory complex. Tobacco factories were notorious fire hazards, and for that very reason, Reynolds installed the best possible sprinkler system available when the original factory was built in 1891. And the system had paid off: Between 1895 and 1899 there were three fires in the building. Each time the sprinkler system extinguished the flames with no lasting damage.[23] During the renovations, the factory sprinkler system had been removed. A new system was being installed, but it was not yet operational when the fire started.

That night, while a new shift of firefighters continued to douse the smoldering remnants of 256, the shell-shocked residents of Albert Hall gathered around the pool at the Hawthorne Inn, where David Shannon had secured them accommodations. They were joined by the owners of the displaced businesses, Shannon, and Jack Steelman. "It was the exact opposite of a confrontational get-together," Steelman said. "The spirit was, 'How do we rise above what's happened and keep going.' ... Everybody really came together and pledged not to let the vision go, but to work even harder and closer together to overcome the adversity and still make the vision become reality.... It really brought out the best in people."[24]

Their determination was shared among community leaders, who, from the day of the fire, were adamant that they would not falter in their efforts to develop a technology economy. Jay Moscowitz of the Wake Forest Medical School said it best: "This community has a lot of fervor to achieve what we're going to achieve. Out of the ashes we will build a research park."[25]

The fire had destroyed four buildings, including the almost completed Frisby Technology Center, and damaged Albert Hall. All the offices in Albert Hall sustained water and smoke damage; some of the condos on the north side, next to the fire, suffered fire damage as well. When the occupants were allowed into the building to briefly collect essential items the day after the fire, they discovered that the heat had melted their computers and anything else made of plastic. Every horizontal surface was coated in ash and the walls were thick with grimy black soot.

The Piedmont Triad Community Research Center sustained minor smoke damage, but was otherwise untouched. However, the loss of power during the fire disrupted a number of experiments in progress.[26]

The community pulled together to help the displaced businesses. Meridian Realty, which was handling the leasing of the old Wachovia Tower on North Main Street, made temporary office space available; the Chamber of Commerce gave them access to telephones, computers and conference rooms.[27] Frisby Technologies, however, was a lost cause. The company wrote off its losses and found new quarters in Greensboro.[28]

At City Hall, Jack Steelman contacted the architect for the research park master plan and had him start revising the plan to show a new building in place of the old tobacco factory.[29] Shannon had already declared his intention to rebuild, but he knew it would be harder to find tenants: Space in renovated old factories could be leased for far less than new construction. And old factories, with their wood floors, high ceilings, and a century's worth of character were a magnet that drew tenants. A new building would hold no such attraction.[30]

Devastating as the fire was, the members of the NCETA board had no choice but to push forward with their agenda. At their meeting on September 18, John McKinnon reported that the executive search firm Heidrick & Struggles had been selected to lead the effort to secure a park director. Jack Steelman reported that the Downtown Development Corp. was well into its preparations to transfer all park property to NCETA. But the best news of all was that, even though the fire had been a great setback, two heartening new developments were moving from the category of "possible" to "probable."[31]

The first was Don Angell's proposed hotel, office building, and parking deck. Angell's plans were beginning to take shape, and were dictating some revisions in the park master plan. The hotel and office building would take up all the city land adjacent to the park, leaving the parking deck to be built across Church Street, within the footprint of the research park campus. The deck would impinge on the southern end of the proposed spec building, necessitating a new alignment for that building within the park. The second heartening development was news that Wachovia had agreed to pre-lease space in the spec building in order to get it under construction, and it would take the lead in working with other banks to complete the financing package for the building.[32]

Don Angell's agreement to build City Hall South (center left), a hotel (lower left), and a parking deck helped spur development of the research park and led to construction of Research One (upper center)   *Photo by Megan Morr, courtesy of Winston-Salem Journal*

Clearly, Alder's recommendation that the city create a broad and powerful committee to implement its technology blueprint was beginning to pay off.

The fall of 1998 saw the NCETA leadership absorbed with its executive search, the minutia of transferring the park property from the DDC to NCETA, Angell's development plans, and developing of a request for proposals for the spec building, which was now being referred to as Research One. More good news came when Gayle Anderson reported in November that the N.C. Technology Development Authority had agreed to the chamber's request to underwrite the cost of a feasibility study to include wet lab space in the spec building. Better yet, the authority indicated that it might be willing to invest in the building.[33]

The first tangible sign of progress came on Jan. 7, 1999, when almost 400 dignitaries, well-wishers, and onlookers gathered for a festive groundbreaking. To the accompaniment of a Moravian band, Mayor Jack Cavanaugh rode in on a forklift and joined 15 other officials in turning the dirt for Angell's $23 million development, which included a 100,000-square-foot office building for the city, a 59,000-square-foot hotel, and a 475-space parking deck.[34] "David Shannon started it," said Angell, referring to the momentum the research park had gained over the past 18 months, "and we're continuing it."[35]

The progress continued. In February the board voted unanimously to hire Bill Dean, and the month after that, it selected Samet Corp to build Research One. The groundbreaking was held March 24.[36]

By the time Dean reported to work on March 26, he was able to take charge of a research park that had shaken off the disastrous fire seven months earlier. Three new buildings and a parking deck were under construction. There was some lingering fallout from the fire, such as Frisby Technology's decision to locate elsewhere rather than wait for space in Research One. But overall, a sense of optimism prevailed.

Dean immediately began working at two levels. On one hand, he dived into the minutia of organizing the park, hiring staff, developing a business plan, and forming a tenants' association. "We had to do everything. It was like starting a business. We had to do our own payroll, do our own health insurance; so for the first year we were building the organization and the business model that we needed to go forward."[37]

At the same time, he was getting to know the local leadership on which the success of the park would depend. "I found myself surrounded in a 10-acre park with small amounts of resources and a land mass to develop," Dean said. "I didn't think that was all bad, because for us to be successful we would have to build a culture. So I started working on developing a culture.... I spent a lot of time making the chicken tour at

Rotary clubs around the community."[38]

Then came the meeting called by Bud Baker to organize the Winston-Salem Alliance, and the dismaying realization that many in the community still did not grasp the research park's potential. After getting over his initial disappointment, Dean decided that he was better off knowing that this was the case. "It really helped me. It helped me because it reaffirmed what I knew from going around to key leaders, talking one on one. It reconfirmed to me the work that needed to be done."[39]

An unexpected item was added to Dean's agenda when the North Carolina Employment and Training Association, established in 1967, notified the newly minted NCETA that it already had claim to the NCETA acronym. Dean told the board members not to be concerned about the prospect of changing the organization's name. As far as he was concerned, it was too cumbersome for effective marketing, anyway.

"So I went to Long Haymes and Carr (advertising agency) and we spent a month re-creating who we are and where were we wanted to go. It was about new ideas and alliances we were putting together, whether public, private, or academic, to carry those ideas forward to ensure the future stability of the economy.... We went through all kinds of names on the wall. They were a very creative group. And out of that they came up with !dealliance, with the exclamation point.

"Then they went to New York as a test, to throw the name out with their own associates: 'What do you think of this?' They did their homework. They took it seriously. They understood for Winston-Salem that this was a serious piece of business."[40]

With the board's assent, the new name was accepted. But by then, Dean's attention was focused elsewhere. Research One was soon to be finished. And it needed a tenant – not Wachovia and its short-term occupancy that enabled the project to move forward – but a real tenant fit for the research park's flagship building. And he had already located that tenant. They just didn't yet know it.

10   TECHNOLOGY FOR ALL

While the events of 1998 were preoccupying the NCETA board members, a complementary technology initiative, long in gestation, was starting to come together. It was called WinstonNet.

The precedent for WinstonNet dated to 10 years earlier, when the medical school arranged to be part of the microwave communications network established by MCNC. But the vision for WinstonNet was far more audacious. Instead of linking Wake Forest University and the medical school to other state institutions of higher education, WinstonNet was envisioned as the city's own internal high-speed computer network linking all the major community institutions – universities and colleges, city and county government, the Winston-Salem/Forsyth County Schools, large corporations, and businesses, households, and non-profit agencies. All would have a super-fast connection to each other and to the Internet.

In many ways, it was a project built on faith. The people working on WinstonNet, among them Jay Dominick, the assistant vice president for information systems at Wake Forest University; David Brown, the director of the International Center for Computer-Enhanced Learning at Wake Forest; and John Boehme, the associate dean for academic computing, could not cite a pressing existing need for wiring the city. But they knew that providing such an infrastructure would lead to good things – and that it was absolutely compatible with the city's efforts to transform its economy. Brown described WinstonNet as "not unlike a community network one thousand times more powerful than the telephone."[1]

With such a network in place, corporations could stream

audio and video, colleges and universities could offer distance learning, government could offer online services to citizens, and businesses could find a wider market, and conversely, find the specialized help they needed through remote workers who lived elsewhere in the country or even the world. All this would make the city and the research park that much more of an attractive place for high-tech companies. Wake Forest and other institutions of higher learning would have a powerful lure in the competition to attract the best faculty members. And the children in Forsyth County would grow up technically savvy and ready to work in the 21st Century.

These outcomes were never envisioned when the initiative that became WinstonNet took shape. It was 1995, and Wake Forest University had made the then-daring decision to issue every student a laptop computer. The Internet was just beginning to reach public consciousness and was growing in popularity daily. University administrators realized that arming every student with a computer would create that much more demand for access to the Internet. The campus was not prepared for this, Boehme said. "We said, 'We don't know what this Internet is, but it's going to be a big thing. We're going to have all these kids on a T-1 line and it's going to be a bottleneck.' So I said, 'We need to do something for ourselves. Let's figure out how to fiber (install fiber-optic cable in) all the buildings on Wake Forest, including the undergraduate campus, the professional schools, and the medical school.'"[2,3]

Wiring all the buildings on campus was a physical challenge in itself; extending the connection to the medical school, separated from the main campus by two miles of residential neighborhoods, made the task considerably more complicated. The fragile glass strands had to be routed through a conduit pipe buried underground, which meant getting permission from every property owner along the route from one campus to the other. Given the need to secure right of way for the conduit, it would take almost two years to complete the connection.[4]

One day, while the university was still working on securing the necessary rights of way, Dallas Mackay asked Boehme to sit in on a meeting of a group called Friends of the Library. Mackay was the university's vice president for development. "The Friends were charged with 'What is the future of the libraries,'" Boehme said. "Dallas asked me to participate because I was involved with technology. So I went to the meeting and there were a lot of past and current Winston-Salem movers and shakers around the table.... One of the things that came out was, 'We have 11 branch libraries. How can we use them?' Well, one thing they could do would be to connect them so they could share resources."

A few days later, at a meeting on the fiber project with Mackay and Jay Dominic, the university's information systems manager, Boehme casually mentioned the Friends' parallel vision of connecting their branch libraries. That sparked some conjecture about someday connecting the county library system to the Z. Smith Reynolds Library on the Reynolda campus, and maybe to the O'Kelly Library on the campus of Winston-Salem State. "One thing led to another in this conversation and we began discussing the idea of using some of the spare fiber for a community network," Boehme said. "So... 'What's a community network?' Well, we didn't know.

"At that time, Wake Forest had a huge relationship with IBM, and they got interested in it and there were some dedicated days when they would come in with their brain trust and talk about community networks." At that early stage, anything seemed possible. "We even talked about how we could have Hanes Mall connected and people could log in to Hanes Mall and see all the sales at all the stores." The conversation was made easier by the fact that Wake Forest was installing two fiber conduits along the network right-of-way – one for its network and a second for future growth.[5]

It was, essentially, the start of WinstonNet, spurred on when Boehme broached the concept with Winston-Salem State. "I was sitting across from Dr. (Alvin) Schexnider (the university chancellor) talking about the possibilities of an interconnection so we could share resources and he said, 'I am not sure what I am agreeing to, but it is something we should do.'"

Next, Boehme approached Forsyth Technical Community College. Marvin Allen, the dean of the business school, was his liaison. At the time the central offices for the Winston-Salem/Forsyth County schools were located next to the FTCC campus. "So Marvin reached out to (Schools Superintendent) Don Martin and said, 'If we can connect (Forsyth Tech), connecting the K-12 system would be easy.'"

In a case of serendipitous timing, these conversations were taking place before the fiber lines had been installed. This presented an opportunity. "John (Anderson), Jay (Dominic), and I said, 'We have to go this route anyway to connect ourselves. Maybe when we get close to Winston-Salem State we can put in a hand-hold.' (A hand-hold is essentially a junction box where a fiber line can be split.) So when we came to Salem or the city or county, we put in hand-holds. We were funding it, but it was the pathway we had to go, anyway.

"Then we said (to these outside entities), 'This is what we are doing. Would you be interested in connecting?' They said, 'Why?' So we started meeting on an ad-hoc basis. Martha Wood was mayor at that time and Gayle (Anderson), Peggy Low (the chamber's technology executive), (City Manager) Bill Stuart, (County Manager) Graham Pervier, and Sam Owen (the city's information systems manager) met and we talked about how do we do this? When do we do it? What's the value of doing it? And the value was, we could share (the cost of) Internet services together." By June 1998, Winston-Salem State, the School of the Arts, Salem College, and Forsyth Tech were formally on board to participate in WinstonNet, to be joined within nine months by the Forsyth County, the city of Winston-Salem, and the Forsyth County Public Libraries.[6,7]

This ability to share the cost of data services established the business case that propelled the initiative forward. It became all the more compelling when the grant expired that had funded Wake Forest's connection to the Microelectronics Center of North Carolina, which tied the university to the Internet. (Wake Forest University's initial connection to the Internet via MCNC was a microwave connection funded by the General Assembly that served both Wake Forest and Winston-Salem State University. That was succeeded by the N.C. Information Highway, which provided a direct T-1 connection between

MCNC and Wake Forest, for which Wake Forest had received a two-year grant that covered the cost of leasing the line.[8])

Fortunately, officials at MCNC had been following the nascent development of WinstonNet and decided to make it the poster child for how they wanted to structure the state's information infrastructure. "MCNC said, 'You're doing what we want all our communities to do,'" Boehme said. "'You have a regional point of presence (a single community connection to the Internet) that is then distributed to local users through a local network.' So they helped fund the connection we had established through the grant. So as the grant ended, the 'RPoP' came online and we never lost our robust speeds. According to them, we were the first RPoP in the state."[9]

MCNC was especially interested in making an example of WinstonNet because it was being overwhelmed by the surging demand for access to the Internet. At the time, every institution and community in North Carolina was connecting directly to MCNC and the growing number of connections was becoming unmanageable. WinstonNet, as a regional point of presence, created a hub-and-spoke model that MCNC saw as the solution: Instead of 20 entities in a community all running their own connections to MCNC, it could run a single connection to the community and the 20 entities would tap in locally.

The government and education leaders who sat in on these early WinstonNet meetings immediately grasped how a local fiber network could advance the community push to use technology to reinvent the local economy. Soon the meetings were discussing how they might use this robust Internet connection to further the revitalization of Winston-Salem. Schools and government could not, of themselves, create new, technology-based jobs in the community. But they could help create the workforce that would attract companies that needed tech-savvy employees. "We could provide computer training and accessibility to people," Boehme said, "to people who did not have computers. And maybe we could be a vehicle to help some people become more skilled in computer technology."

With all hands backing the initiative, and given its clear implications for the city's overall technology efforts, WinstonNet was added to the portfolio of projects under NCETA's purview.[10]

For the Winston-Salem/Forsyth County Schools, the advent of WinstonNet came at a propitious moment. For more than a year, the schools – with financial backing from the Chamber of Commerce – had been working with a consultant to develop a strategic technology plan for the school system. Under a partnership with Wake Forest University, the school system was slated to receive some 800 used laptop computers every year, but the system was ill-prepared for such largess.[11]

The consultant, Brennan/Levinson Enterprise of Washington, D.C., was to bring coherence to the school system's haphazard employment of technology across its 45 campuses that served more than 35,000 students. Each school had authority over its technology, or lack thereof, including its selection of hardware, software, and operating systems. The more ambitious – or better funded – schools averaged one computer per classroom, and there were no electronic links between the school system's central office and the administrative offices for the individual schools. School secretaries downloaded their information to diskettes that were sent to the central office by interoffice mail, to be transferred to central office databases. The hodgepodge of hardware and software made interoperability all but impossible. The state had developed comprehensive K-12 proficiency standards to be assessed during eighth grade, but systematic instruction to those standards was lacking. "There is a crash-course attempt in the eighth grade to teach the skills," the consultant noted, "but many of the teachers do not have the technology skills required to teach the material effectively."[12]

Other shortcomings the consultant noted: "There is no district-wide effort (to integrate technology into the curriculum) and instructional services still focus on printed matter."…"There is little training for administrators in the management of technology, and only a few schools have technology coordinators."… "The (school system's) Department of Instruction's expertise is a print-based curriculum and is not software-based."

However, there was a silver lining in this state of affairs.

"The lack of technology infrastructure, legacy systems, and technological equity within the schools invites opportunity, as there is little resistance to change. The schools can leapfrog the current instructional delivery system and use the new, networked technology as a central tool to improve standards-based performance on statewide testing and provide students with the technology-based skills they will need for higher education entry-level jobs."[13]

Thanks to WinstonNet and the partnership with Wake Forest, the school system had the opportunity to become a national leader in the integration of technology into the teaching and learning process. The end result, as envisioned in the consultant's report, would be schools with a computer for every four students, networked to each other and to a server in the school that in turn would be networked to servers in the school system's central office. All teachers would have laptop computers with remote access for working at home. Instructional materials would be delivered over these networks, and students would be taught with a mix of textbooks, web-based instructional packages, simulations, and instructional software.[14]

In this vision, technology and curriculum would be synonymous. In mathematics, technology would be used to graphically see and illustrate mathematical concepts and results. Upper-level students would use spreadsheets, graphs, charts, and databases to collect, organize, and analyze data, and draw conclusions. Students would begin using computers for word-processing by the second grade and would be able to make multi-media presentations by the sixth grade. School media centers, and their staffs, would play a crucial role in this technology revolution. The school network would allow students and teachers to access media center materials directly from their classrooms, and the media center staff would become electronic infrastructure specialists, responsible for managing their schools' technology resources and obtaining network-based electronic information.[15]

To achieve this transformation, the consultant laid out a five-year transition plan and called for a reorganization of the central office staff. To coordinate and standardize the adoption

of technology the schools should designate an assistant superintendent of technology and create a department of technology that would oversee infrastructure, applications and support,
and assist each school's technology efforts.

WinstonNet was key to achieving this, and the consultant
recommended that the school district start actively participating in this effort. The bandwidth and speed of WinstonNet gave
the school system the opportunity to provide instructional
materials and management systems over the network. "This
would permit the district to leapfrog all the other school systems in the country and become a leader in the use of technology for education."[16]

All the databases needed for instruction and management
could be kept on distributed servers that would be connected
and accessed by WinstonNet. Software could reside on the web
and be accessed through web browsers, making it easy for students, staff, and teachers to access the software from any web-
connected computer. To provide the requisite high-speed access
to make this possible, each school building could be connected
to WinstonNet by a high-bandwidth fiber-optic conduit.

Perhaps the most challenging aspect of the entire effort
would be bringing teachers, administrators, and support staff
up to speed in this new technology-centered environment. The
school system was in the habit of spending about seven percent
of its technology budget on training. In the private sector, this
figure was often 50 percent. At a minimum, the consultant
suggested that the school system plan on upping its training
budget to at least 30 percent of its total technology budget. The
money would be spent both for formal training, establishment
of a help desk, and informal mentoring and coaching in the
schools.[17]

Teachers, especially, would have to get up to speed if the
vision of a new, technology-driven curriculum was to be realized. Teachers would be the target of training courses, work-
shops, ongoing in-school training, and peer coaching. In a
reverse of the status quo – in which the hardware was installed
and the teacher left to learn how to use it – the consultant
recommended that teachers be required to complete a training

course and demonstrate basic competence before getting access to hardware or software. "This policy will facilitate immediate classroom use, minimize downtime, and increase overall satisfaction with technology."[18]

Beyond the initial push to bring teachers up to speed, the school system would also have to put in place a protocol for ongoing training that would keep teachers current with newer versions of software and hardware. "Thoroughly integrating technology into training and learning is a three- to five-year process. The main tasks are to reengineer the instruction process, adapt students and teachers to a new medium of instructional materials, and expand the teaching repertoire to encompass technology-based methods and approaches. This transformation will take considerable time, management, and organization.[19]

"Technology will be so integrated into all subject matter that it will be difficult to distinguish the subject matter from the technology." Once accomplished, however, the technology transformation would amount to a revolution in the classroom – one that would prepare students for the new, technology-driven economy that city leaders were working to bring about.

To ensure that teachers and students would have adequate computers to accomplish these ambitious goals, the chamber took the lead in organizing an $8 million private sector campaign called "Touched by Technology," and helped get $15 million in public funding for technology included in a 2001 bond referendum for the schools. The chamber then led the business community in promoting passage of the bonds.[20] For its efforts the chamber received the 2003 "Friend of Education" award from the North Carolina Association for Supervision and Curriculum. The award honors individuals and organizations who have made contributions in education through visionary and committed leadership.[21]

As the education blueprint was moving forward, Bill Dean was working through his initial "to-do" list at the research park. Among those items was putting together a tenant association for the companies in the park. "We wanted as an organization to do everything we could to allow these companies to come to this park and be sustained and grow," Dean said. "There's nothing better when recruiting than to have a CEO or a president say, 'This park helped me succeed.' So I wanted to know what's going on. While I didn't have control of these companies, I didn't want to be surprised with failures, and if we could do anything to help avoid failures, we needed to do this. We didn't need to have any losses as we moved forward in creating the culture and the community buy-in. And we had a lot of young start-ups and I was nervous about this."[22]

"So at the first meeting we had cookies and we wanted to tell them what !dealliance is: This is our business model; we want to hear from you. To my surprise there were still some sore feelings about the fire and probably, as with any entrepreneur, the feeling of 'I'm out here by myself.'... And they were saying, 'I don't know if this is going to work.' I said, 'Guys, give me a chance. This is what I want to know.'"

"One person said, 'We're going to get together and we're all going to move out.' I said, 'That's the wrong thing to do.' And I said, 'I know where you're coming from. I've financed start-up companies as a banker.' I said, 'Stick with us and let us build it together. If you go out on your own there's no net. We're going to build a net and we're going to do this together. You're far better off in a group that understands the process than out on your own.' So we calmed their anxiety level, but that put the onus on us."[23]

Completion of the Technology One building in the summer of 2000 put on the front burner another challenge: finding a long-term tenant for the building. Wachovia was leasing two floors of the building for its recently formed e-commerce division, an accommodation that fulfilled the crucial pre-leasing quota for construction. But Wachovia didn't want to stay there, and Dean didn't want them to stay. He wanted a true research company in the park's new flagship building. And he knew just which company it should be. So he picked up the phone and made an appointment with Don DeBethizy, a vice president for research and development at R.J. Reynolds.

DeBethizy had joined Reynolds in 1985 as a research scientist in its nascent nicotine research group. By 2000 the group had grown from a handful of people to 23 full-time researchers investigating ways to make benevolent use of the brain's nicotine receptors. "A group developing the first Alzheimer's therapies came to us, asking if we had a safe drug that interacted with the nicotine receptors in the brain," DeBethizy said, "because it was beginning to be known that was a potential target for treating Alzheimer's patients....

"It seemed that if you could eliminate some of the side effects of nicotine, such as increased heart and blood pressure, nausea and addiction, you could conceive that you might be able to develop new chemicals that could target subtypes for memory."[24]

Construction of Research One, the first new building to go up in the Research Park, was made possible when Wachovia agreed to pre-lease two floors as temporary housing for its e-commerce division. *Photo by Frank Elliott*

By the time Bill Dean made his appointment, Reynolds had spun off Targacept as a separate company. "They were cutting expenses, paying off debt (from the leveraged buyout) and so the environment had changed," DeBethizy said. "We were a great idea and a real big opportunity, but it was off-purpose to a company that really had to focus on its mission."

Reynolds gave the company temporary quarters in an old building at its research campus next to the Whitaker Park factory, and a deal with Aventis kept the company alive while it pursued venture capital to continue operations. Targacept succeeded in raising $30.4 million in venture capital, but needed to find permanent space. The venture capitalists funding the company wanted it to move to an area with an established biotech sector, such as San Diego, Boston, Austin, or Research Triangle Park. DeBethizy was even fielding offers from other countries interested in luring the promising startup.

Over lunch at a nearby restaurant, Dean made the pitch for having Targacept move into the research park. "I wanted them to be an anchor," Dean said, "a home-grown company.... So as we were beginning to discuss where and how to put Don in the park, we focused on the One Technology building."[26]

DeBethizy was receptive to the idea. As a graduate of Leadership Winston-Salem, he was socially invested in the community, and as a former adjunct professor at the Bowman Gray School of Physiology and Pharmacology, he was friends with Jim Smith, the department head. Now that Smith's school was in the old Quality Assurance building, DeBethizy was very interested in working near him.[27] "There's a tremendous synergy we can garner from just being in close proximity to the pharmacology researchers," he told Piedmont Triad Business after the move. "Our major deals were in Europe, and we've been recruited by places like Munich, Germany. But Winston-Salem has made a serious commitment to building a biotech sector."[28]

The One Technology building, with its combination of office and wet lab space, was perfectly suited for DeBethizy's needs. The fact that it was just a shell was a positive, in some respects, because DeBethizy had definite opinions about the impression his offices needed to convey. "When people come off that elevator, I want them to be impressed and say, 'This is a company to invest in; to work for; to be a part of in a collateral way.'"[29] But because it was just a shell, it would take a lot of money to outfit the labs as he needed. And that was the rub: Targacept could not spend any of the venture capital it had raised on a building or other capital costs, and it had little other money to pay for the upfit. "He only had X amount of dollars to do it with," Dean said. "I said, 'What is the gap we need to raise?' It was close to $5 million. So I said, 'OK, how are we going to do this?'"[30]

Don DeBethizy in his new quarters in Research One, which soon came to be known as the Targacept Building.
Photo by David Sandler, courtesy of Winston-Salem Journal

Dean became preoccupied with finding a way to get Targacept into the park. He discussed the issue with Bob Leak at Winston-Salem Business Inc., the city's business recruiting agency, and with the Chamber of Commerce. A delegation including Leak, Dean, and chamber representatives went to Raleigh to discuss the issue with the Department of Commerce and to the Research Triangle Park to meet with the North Carolina Biotechnology Center. "We went to anybody and everybody we could go to," Dean said. "And I said, 'Guys, you've got to give me something.' One of the guys in Raleigh threw a dime on the table and I snapped it up. 'I'll take it!' That's a true story. We reported back to the !dealliance board: Here's the gap, and there was a hush. And I was getting worried about how to manage the gap so I met with Tom (Hearn) and Dick (Dean) and I remember the conversation quite well.

"I said, 'This is going to be detrimental and a turning point. Can you imagine the message this is going to send? We're trying to develop a research park and we can't even take care of our own?' And my remark was, 'If we can't do this, we might as well fold up our tent and go home.'"[31]

Further talks with Dick Dean presented Bill Dean with the opportunity to meld his goal of landing Targacept with another priority he had set for the park. "To me, if we didn't build a cluster of technologies and springboard off of that we would not become a true research park. A lot of people in this business will tend to make it a real estate deal and it's not. Real estate is only necessary to house the technology.

"So I wanted to take that chamber blueprint and build a cluster of technologies. Then I had a meeting with Dick Dean and I said, 'We need a focus. How can we get more of Wake Forest Health Sciences down into the park?' The quick response was they had a nutrition building on the Hawthorne campus to fill up.... Dick said, 'Bill, what do you want?' I said, 'I want to build clusters of leading technologies that we can move into the park and springboard off that so we have things that can come out of here and attract others.'"[32]

The seed that Bill Dean had planted in that earlier conversation bore fruit as he was grasping for a way to raise money for Targacept. "I went to Dick and told him that I had talked to BB&T. They said they would loan him the money and help Targacept if we had someone with money to guarantee the loan. !dealliance couldn't do that." But, he said, the medical school could. "I said, 'Dick, the reason I say this is if Targacept fails you have enough backlog of need for lab space that you can fill that building.' He said, 'Bill, why would I want to do that? If I can do this (guarantee the loan)...I'll just buy the building.' And that was the trigger. Dick took the lead and structured a lease with Targacept that fit its needs.

"This was a turning point for me, a turning point in that it brought in technology from a home-grown company to demonstrate to community that, yes, we can do it. And now we had a CEO in the park who was not only a tech CEO but who could be a cheerleader as well. The other significant thing was, now Wake Forest Health Sciences had another building in the park."[33]

And soon the medical school would be in a third building, too. David Shannon had been working to find tenants for the new building he planned to put up to replace what was to have been the Frisby Technology Center. It had been slow going. Frisby Technology, which was to have been his anchor tenant in the old building, had found quarters in Greensboro, leaving Shannon in the same no-man's-land that had stymied efforts to build Technology One. Until he had an anchor tenant he could not get financing to put up a new building. But most prospective tenants were small companies without the wherewithal to lease a significant amount of space. And the larger prospects were more interested in shell space that offered a faster timeline to occupancy.

Wake Forest again supplied the solution. Shannon approached the medical school about moving its Physician's Assistant program to the proposed building – an offer made palatable by the competitive rent Shannon proposed to charge. It presented a lower-cost option for freeing up space on Hawthorne Hill than some other alternatives, and having the program a half-block from the pharmacology/physiology department in the park would simplify logistical support. On April 7, 2000, Shannon announced that he would start construction of a new 40,000-square-foot building that month and that the Wake Forest Physician's Assistant program would occupy 13,400 square feet. The building was to be called Victoria Hall.[34]

With these developments, the seeds were planted for what would become a dramatic new direction for the research park.

11 REBOOTING

Pete Santago well remembers a meeting in the early 1990s with Larry Monteith, the chancellor of NC State, during the push to establish the Piedmont Triad Engineering Research Center. "His comment was, 'You need tenacity. You have to sink your teeth into it.'" In the spring of 2000, Santago was realizing just how right Monteith had been, given the struggles to create a viable engineering presence in Winston-Salem. In theory, that need was being filled by PTERC. But the theory had not been fulfilled in practice. PTERC was on life support, and fading fast.[1]

The issue was money. The $3 million appropriation that the General Assembly approved in 1993 provided $500,000 for computers, networking equipment, and other infrastructure the center needed. "But," Santago said, "we couldn't spend it on ongoing costs; we couldn't hire people." And even this amount rubbed some folks the wrong way, as witnessed by the very public objections UNC Vice President Jasper Memory had raised about the appropriation.[2]

Despite the headwind coming out of Chapel Hill, Santago, who had been appointed interim director of the center, spent most of 1994 trying to get PTERC off the ground. The "to-do" list was seemingly endless, ranging from selecting research projects and recruiting researchers, to such mundane chores as arranging for signs, stationery, and telephones.

PTERC was conceived as a collaboration, primarily between NC State and Wake Forest, along with NC A&T and UNC-Greensboro. But institutional rivalry, coupled with residual resentment over the genesis of PTERC, was slowing the process at every turn. Santago's notes from a meeting with the UNC administration in November 1994 are representative:

137

"Considerable negatives indicated, especially in
the realm of handling off-campus faculty – promo-
tions, other duties, etc.... The people 'downtown'
(i.e. the NC State administration) wanted to know
why the responsibilities of PTERC couldn't just be
done at RTP.... My comment was that PTERC had
been endorsed by the UNC board as a way to extend
engineering expertise and that NCSU should find a
way to do this. I also detected a considerable reluctance to deal with the other state school members.
They consider this political overhead and unnec-
essary."[3]

Santago persevered though the delays and second-guessing
and eventually PTERC got up and running, based out of the
Piedmont Triad Community Research Center on Chestnut
Street. By 1996, several graduate students, including some at
NC A&T, were enrolled and pursuing research. But the center
never progressed beyond having a handful of participants. "We
offered classes here, and we received them here (via distance
learning links) but we couldn't push it enough to keep it moving," Santago said. "We were never flying on State's radar."[4]

The failure of PTERC to thrive left the medical center back
where it started: still trying to establish a robust engineering
program to complement its medical research. This was the status quo when Santago attended a conference in Northern
Virginia on biomedical engineering organized by the Whitaker
Foundation. "I happened to be up there and I ran into Wally
Grant. He was at Virginia Tech and we started talking about
stuff and he seemed to think, 'We could do something together. We have a big engineering school, you have the medical
school; we need each other.' Usually you just talk about it and
it goes away. But it didn't. I got an invitation to go up and give
a talk about what we were doing.... We got to talking and said,
'We need a joint program of some sort.'"[5]

With interest sufficiently piqued, Grant, a professor of engineering science and mathematics, and Elaine Scott, a professor
of mechanical engineering, paid a reciprocal visit to Winston-

Salem to meet with Wake Forest administrators. This was followed by several months of follow-up meetings and emails to produce the framework of a collaboration that they could take to their respective leadership.[6]

As Santago and Grant saw it, a partnership could help the institutions advance their mutual aspirations to increase their national statures. An executive summary of a proposed joint program noted that Charles Steger, the president of Virginia Tech, had just challenged his university to place within the top 30 research universities in the United States by 2010. "Virginia Tech's 2000 Annual Report noted that only 6 percent of the university's funding came from DHHS (the Department of Health and Human Services) (including NIH), a traditionally underused resource at VT," the summary noted. "Considering that only one of the top 30 research institutions in the

When PTERC fizzled out, Pete Santago led Wake Forest's efforts to create a joint biomedical engineering program with Virginia Tech.
Photo courtesy of Pete Santago

United States does not have a medical school or a BME (biomedical engineering) program and that over 90 percent of the top 40 colleges of engineering have a BME program, being able to access this funding is critical to VT's goals."[7]

Similarly, the executive summary noted that Wake Forest had identified seven strategic goals: "Three of these goals are pertinent to the BME initiatives: to rank within the top 20 recipients of NIH direct research funding and to have at least 10 programs in the top 10 of their area of study, to rank within the top 20 recipients in total extramural research funding, and to rank within the top 30 academic health centers in annual licensing revenue. Currently, all of the top 20 NIH-funded institutions have an engineering school or BME department, and most have both."[8]

A tie-up with Wake Forest was all the more compelling for Virginia Tech because it had just started, in the fall of 1998, a Center for Biomedical Engineering to pursue funded research in biomedical engineering. The executive summary explained that Wake Forest could offer the embryonic center "affiliation with a top-50 medical school that ranks 40th among 123 U.S. medical schools in NIH funding, a medical center with top-50 rankings in 10 of 16 specialties, close proximity, and a wide range of research interests, such as aging, genomics, cancer, pulmonary diseases, women's health, stroke, hypertension and diabetes."[9]

In return, Virginia Tech could offer Wake Forest expertise "in numerous related research areas, including fiber and electro-options, human factors engineering, composite materials and structures, wireless telecommunications and smart materials," the summary noted. "Strong research programs related to BME are found throughout the university and include polymer chemistry, biochemistry and molecular biology, the Center for Gerontology and the Virginia Bioinfomatics Institute. Finally, the Virginia-Maryland Regional College of Veterinary Medicine, located at VT, has the capabilities for testing and monitoring advanced biomedical technologies in animals before their application to human patients."[10]

Perhaps most important of all, 13 departments at the Wake Forest University Baptist Medical Center had committed a total of $1.5 million to fund for the first three years a Wake Forest University Center for Biomedical Engineering as a counterpoint to Virginia Tech's Center for Biomedical Engineering. "I thought that bode well, and that's what early on enabled us to do it on this side," Santago said.[11]

Having made a compelling case for a joint program, the next step was to secure the blessing of the leadership of the respective institutions. Arrangements were made for Dr. Richard Dean, who had succeeded Richard Janeway as president of the medical center in 1997, to meet with the senior administrators in Blacksburg. "We met at Smith Reynolds Airport," Santago said. "It was Doug Maynard, Dick Dean, and me. It was horrible weather. The Virginia Tech plane was going to pick us up from Radford, but the plane couldn't get down. What do we do now? We really needed to do this. Doug (mischievously) didn't skip a beat. He said, 'Dick, Pete says he'll drive.' Dick is from Radford. He knew his way around there so he took us up on all the back roads.

"So we got up there and had a meeting with all the big shots. People were sitting around in groups. I could hear the engineers saying we want to this and that. Then President (Charles) Steger, the president of Virginia Tech, came in and sat down. He said, 'This is a good idea. We're going to do it.' So all the deans there bought into it. Their attitude before was, 'This is a good idea (in theory), but it's one more thing to have to get done.'"[12]

These discussions were formalized by a Memorandum of Understanding between the two universities, signed on December 21, 2001, to pursue "a mutually beneficial arrangement which may lead to a formal collaboration agreement and joint degree programs offered by both institutions." The MOU specifically committed the schools to pursue "mutual cooperation and exchange in the field of biomedical engineering and sciences," to include joint research, faculty, and student exchanges, development of joint degree programs "and/or development of a joint school of biomedical engineering and sciences."[13]

"Steger came down and he met with Tom Hearn over lunch," Santago said. "I got to sit at the end of the table like the little children at the table with the adults, and it was interesting. They signed the MOU and we listened to them bemoaning the state of their sports teams."[14]

Having agreed in principle to create a joint program, it fell to Santago and his counterparts at Virginia Tech to work out the details of what would be called the Virginia Tech-Wake Forest University School of Biomedical Engineering and Sciences. For Santago, it was previously trod ground, for many of the issues were similar to those he had grappled with in establishing PTERC, including devising an academic and administrative structure for the school, faculty appointments, admission and enrollment procedures, research pursuits, and a policy for sharing patents, grants, indirect costs, and intellectual property.[15]

"There were a lot of details we needed to work out," Santago said. "We said, 'We need to get the financial people, the intellectual property people, the academics, together. Let's find (a place to meet) between the two.' So we got a meeting room in a hotel in Wytheville (Va.) and they brought sandwiches in and by the time we left we had every issue worked out....

"Every step of the way we never hit anybody who said it's a bad idea. It can't get done. We had no problem with little things like the order of the names (i.e. which school would be listed first). Up there things are called colleges; here they're schools. That was no problem. We need to create a joint diploma. No problem." [16]

The red tape was particularly thick in Virginia, because Virginia Tech is a state institution, Santago said. "Elaine did the real yeoman's work. She did a huge amount of bureaucratic work, particularly in dealing with the state of Virginia.... First it had to go through the Board of Visitors for Tech. Then it had to go to the Virginia State Council of Higher Education."[17]

While the formal agreement worked its way through the bureaucracy, the two schools started working together informally. By the fall of 2002, about 20 students were taking graduate engineering courses in biomedical engineering, signaling, and mammalian physiology, the latter coming as something of a surprise to the engineering-minded students in Blacksburg. "Teaching physiology to biomedical engineering students is absolutely essential," Santago said. "They must be able to meld biology and engineering."[18]

Additionally, seven departments at the medical center had already embarked on collaborative engineering-related research projects. They included development of implantable springs for the treatment of craniostenosis and development of sensory wireless devices to measure physiological functions within mouse models. One project for Orthopaedics involved 19 students. The two faculties divided the teaching duties through distance learning, even though the program had yet to be advertised because, officially, it did not yet exist.[19] The joint school was made practical in large part by the continuing improvements in distance learning equipment, allowing for simultaneous video and computer display. For example, by using a special pen, an instructor could mark up slides and illustrations on the computer screen, or write directly on a blank screen, creating virtual white boards seen simultaneously on both campuses. Improvements in teleconferencing made it easier to hold virtual faculty meetings.[20]

The alacrity with which the Wake Forest departments jumped into the program did not surprise Santago. "A great part of medicine is technology-driven. It's devices or implants or imaging modalities or machines for monitoring vital signs. They knew that medicine is very much tied to technology and technology is tied to engineering."[21]

The enthusiasm was matched in Blacksburg. After Doug Maynard attended his first meeting as a member of the Advisory Board of the College of Engineering at Virginia Tech, he reported, "I was quite impressed with the support that exists for the joint program between our two schools.... At a time when Virginia Tech is absorbing huge budget cuts as a result of the state of Virginia's economic situation, these programs have nevertheless received full support."[22]

In all, it would take 15 months to work through the administrative process and get the joint program officially sanctioned – without which the program could not award degrees to its graduates. In North Carolina, the program had to be approved by the UNC Board of Governors – even though Wake Forest is a private institution – in order for Virginia Tech to operate in the state. That approval cleared the board on Feb. 14, 2003. The following month, the program came for final approval before the State Council for Higher Education in Virginia, so that Wake Forest could operate there.

"Periodically they hold their meetings at various colleges," Santago said. "This one was at Sweet Briar. So I went up there and we were on the agenda. It was presented and there were only two comments. One was, 'How much is this going to cost?' And the next was, 'This is the kind of thing that we need to be doing.'"[23] On March 19, 2003, it became official.

"Steger's vision was, 'Over time there will be some major players in university research and they will be defined by those who are working together.' So we got that signed. And then we did the single most important thing that establishes you in the modern world: We made a website."[24]

The program was an immediate success. The inaugural year saw 20 graduate applications and admissions, but the number of applicants soared in the ensuring years, to 70 in 2004, 120 in 2006, and 220 by 2012, still competing for 20 to 30 available seats each year.[25]

Establishment of the joint biomedical engineering program – and its subsequent growth into a thriving component of its host universities – finally fulfilled Doug Maynard's goal, first outlined almost 20 years earlier, of bringing engineering to Winston-Salem. Along the way, the pursuit of that goal laid the foundation for a transformative shift, not only in Winston-Salem's economy, but in the city's image of itself. For generations, city residents had found civic pride in Winston-Salem's manufacturing prowess, but more importantly, had found in its factories the means for a comfortable livelihood. The layoffs of the 1980s broke that social contract, and gave rise to the efforts that forged a new economic base for the city.

As with any transformation, the vision evolved. What started as a quest for an engineering school expanded into an awareness that future generations of workers would not be able to count on finding a job in a tobacco factory or a knitting mill, which in turn led to the notion of harnessing the research at Bowman Gray Medical School to create companies that could create replacement jobs. These new employers would need a place to do business, and so the vision expanded again to include a research park. As this refined vision gained traction among the city's leaders it gave rise to a community-wide effort to embrace technology as the foundation for a new economic model that would sustain Winston-Salem in the 21st century. This would require both infrastructure and skills, and thus was born WinstonNet, the K-12 Blueprint for Technology and soon, creation of new curriculum and programs at Forsyth Technical Community College.

Throughout this evolution the original quest for engineering proceeded in fits and false starts until a lasting solution was found through the partnership with Virginia Tech. By the time that partnership was producing its first graduates, events had borne out the wisdom of working to build a new economic foundation. The layoffs that had dropped Reynolds Tobacco to 7,000 local employees in 1990 continued unabated throughout the years of creating a research park and its related initiatives. By 2007, Reynolds would have only 2,100 local employees. Sara Lee dropped from 6,600 employees to 4,000, while spinning off Hanesbrands in the process. Wachovia Bank and Trust merged with First Union, which in turn merged with Wells Fargo, exporting yet more jobs. However, medicine – the horse to which the community had hitched its technology wagon – was picking up the slack. Over the same period employment at Wake Forest Baptist Medical Center had more than doubled to

Dr. Douglas Maynard speaks at the unveiling of a sculpture in the research park, created to recognize his leadership in fomenting the city's technology transformation.

Photo by Teesha McClam, courtesy of Winston-Salem Journal

11,400 and Novant had grown from 5,300 to 7,500.

And still the vision evolved. Seven months before all the requisite agencies signed off on the Virginia Tech-Wake Forest University School of Biomedical Engineering and Sciences, the pursuit of technology took a dramatically ambitious turn with the announcement in August 2002 that Wake Forest Health Sciences was assuming management of the research park and massively expanding its footprint to encompass the entire eastern flank of downtown Winston-Salem. Technology was here to stay.

EPILOGUE

It was a typical August day, hot and humid, when Dr. Richard Dean, the president and CEO of Wake Forest University Health Sciences, took to the podium under a massive canopy set up in a parking lot next to the Community Research Building. Before him sat more than 200 movers and shakers from throughout Winston-Salem and North Carolina who had responded to the invitation to attend an announcement about the future of the research park. Within the audience, speculation about exactly what was to be announced could only have been heightened by the caliber of the dignitaries sharing the dais; among them U.S. Rep. Richard Burr, N.C. Commerce Secretary James T. Fain, Mayor Allen Joines, RJR CEO Andrew Schindler, Wake Forest President Thomas Hearn, and Chancellor Harold Martin of Winston-Salem State.[1]

The announcement lived up to the list of speakers. To the accompaniment of the theme from "Star Wars," Dean unveiled plans for a dramatic re-imagining of the scope of the Piedmont Triad Research Park that would take it from 10 acres to nearly 200.[2] Although there were few specifics in the announcement, the aerial photo showing the land identified for the park expansion was sufficiently impressive. Compared to the current footprint of the park, the huge swath of land designated for the expansion was so much larger than the original park that it begged credibility. It literally flanked all of downtown Winston-Salem, stretching from Seventh Street on the north to Salem Creek on the south, and encompassing everything east of downtown to U.S. 52.

In his remarks, Dean acknowledged the responsibility that the medical center was assuming with the expansion. "This plan represents a major commitment to transform our economy from one driven by manufacturing to one led by technology," he said.[3] "We anticipate that as this park reaches maturity over the next 10 to 15 years, it can mean more than 10,000 new jobs, around $5 million in annual property tax revenues alone, and over $2.5 billion in total economic impact for the entire region."[4] In comparison, at the time about 600 people were working in the park with a total payroll of almost $25 million.[5]

Dr. Richard Dean, center, chatting before the park expansion announcement on Aug. 13, 2002. Under Dean's leadership, Wake Forest Health Sciences became the guiding force in the direction and development of the park.
Photo by Jennifer Rotenizer, courtesy of Winston-Salem Journal

At its essence, the impetus for expanding the park was geography. In realizing Dick Janeway's goal of elevating the medical center into the ranks of the NIH's top-40 funded medical centers, Wake Forest had created a space crunch on Hawthorne Hill that could not be solved by grafting yet more high-rise towers onto the existing Ardmore location.[6] The only practical solution was to establish a satellite campus. And, given that the medical center had already established a presence downtown in the Community Research Building and Research One, it made sense to start downtown, said Graydon Pleasants, a consultant who facilitated Targacept's move into Research One and later would oversee the park's real-estate acquisitions.

"The challenge was, 'Can we identify 40 acres for a second campus somewhere downtown near the research park,'" Pleasants said.[7] Of course, there were 40 acres – and more – to be had, immediately to the east of the research park on the other side of the railroad tracks. It was a jumble of parcels bounded by Third Street, U.S. 52, Business 40, and Patterson and Salem avenues. The area had played a pivotal role in the initial industrialization of the town of Winston in the 1870s when the Richmond and Danville Railroad made it the western terminus of a spur line that connected Winston to the North Carolina Railroad main line in Greensboro. Soon the single track gave way to a bustling rail yard as entrepreneurs like Thomas Brown, Pleasant Hanes, and Richard Reynolds built tobacco warehouses and factories in Winston to take advantage of the railroad. Later, Norfolk and Western built a competing rail yard next to the first, further spurring the rapid industrialization of Winston in the late 19th century.

During the latter half of the 20th century the rail yards gave way to other commercial and industrial uses, among them a bus terminal, a plumbing supply company, a dry cleaning plant, a construction company, and an automotive repair business. Although the owners of those businesses would probably have not agreed, it seemed clear to the research park visionaries that the city would be better served if this land were part of the research park. But it would take some doing to make the area work: All told, the land they had identified was held by 16 different owners and home to seven businesses. Further complicating the picture, it also contained high-voltage electric transmission lines, railroad tracks that were still active, and a cell phone tower, all of which would have to be relocated.[8]

Another complication was the concrete plant on the south side of Business 40, immediately across from the tracts the medical center was eyeing. The plant spewed out copious amounts of dust and was utterly incompatible with the image of a high-tech research park. Dean, however, saw this as an opportunity to think even bigger. Instead of confining itself to the tracts immediately east of the research park, the medical center could include the land south of Business 40, all the way down to Salem Creek. And instead of building a satellite campus, they could create a much larger research park that would happen to include their satellite campus – and still accommodate other tech uses as well as any expansion needs of Winston-Salem State and Salem College.

But Dean's vision was bigger still. At a meeting to discuss the footprint for the proposed park expansion, Dean suggested that they consider including all the under-used industrial tracts stretching as far north as Martin Luther King Jr. Drive. Pleasants responded with a simple question: "How big is your appetite for complexity?"[9]

If the park stretched all the way south to Salem Creek, it would displace the City Yard, a sprawling 50-acre complex of buildings, shops, warehouses, and heavy-equipment lots that was home to most of the city of Winston-Salem's public works divisions, including Streets, Sanitation, Transportation, Vegetation Management, Property Management, Fleet Services, and Field Engineering.

Like the concrete plant, the City Yard was incompatible with the research park and separated the park from Winston-Salem State and Salem College. City Manager Bill Stuart was cool to the idea because of the expense of moving the yard and all its infrastructure, even if a suitable location could be found.[10] The medical center received a more sympathetic hearing from Allen Joines, who had retired as deputy city manager in December 2000 and was elected mayor in 2001. Joines understood that the expansion would greatly benefit the city's employment and tax bases in the long run and said he would remain open to the idea if the logistics could be worked out.

North of Third Street, the landholdings were dominated by Reynolds Tobacco and its all-but-abandoned downtown production complex. The area included four massive five- and six-story industrial buildings originally built between 1916 and 1960 as factories and warehouses. It also included the old coal-fired power plant Reynolds built in 1922 to power them all.[11]

Dean had sound tactical reasons for thinking on such a grand scale. "With the city going in the direction it was going, I believed that we needed to expand beyond our needs to address the community's needs. And the larger the audience that would benefit from this initiative the greater the likelihood of it being successful.... Any time you can get independent parties that – from their perspective – will benefit from one initiative, you end up with a critical mass that won't let it die."[12]

As this new vision for the research park was coming into focus, R.J. Reynolds found yet another opportunity to assist the city's technology transformation. Having already sold at discount the Quality Assurance building to the medical school and transferred the ill-fated Factory 256 complex to the county, Reynolds let the Medical Center have the factory complex north of Third Street that Dean had identified as part of a possible park expansion. Nonetheless, the offer raised a few eyebrows at the medical center, Pleasants said. "If someone is going to offer you 30 acres and 2 million square feet, you have to see if you can digest it."[13]

To help make sense of this new vision, medical center officials sent a request for proposals to design firms that had experience working on large-tract site plans, five of whom were invited to the Graylyn Conference Center to pitch their proposals in person.[14]

The job went to Sasaki Associates Inc., a planning and design firm headquartered in Watertown, Mass. "It was within minutes of Dan (Kenny, of Sasaki) talking about the work they had done and the places they had done, that they had the inside advantage," said Doug Edgeton, Wake Forest Health Science's senior vice president for finance and administration. "They were into environmental issues ahead of most people. We knew that was important in order to redevelop that land downtown, that things like LEED were coming and so when they talked about how they try to recycle and reuse and do things that are environmentally friendly, we knew they were the right group."[15,16]

Drawing up a plan would prove to be the easy part. Gaining actual control of all the component tracks within the footprint of the expansion was far more difficult. The initial overtures to the property owners were met with more than a few grains of salt, Pleasants said. "It took a lot to get past that initial skepticism with these property owners. There are plenty of people who hire a planner, and the planned development goes well beyond the property owned by their client, and it's aspirational.... Over the years they had heard different people with different visions approach them and nothing had come of it – and most of these deals come with contingencies. We were able to approach them with the credibility of (Wake Forest) Health Sciences. That, and the fact that we were willing to pay cash, made the difference."[17]

But it took a concerted effort just to locate everyone they needed to reach in order to make their pitch. More often than not, it seemed that the people they needed to engage were in other cities. Duke Power was headquartered in Charlotte, Greyhound was in Dallas, Dillon Supply was in Raleigh, Noland Building Company was based in Newport News, VA, Norfolk Southern was in Norfolk, VA, and Piedmont Natural Gas was in Charlotte. Perhaps the most difficult to deal with was the 40-year-old concrete plant on the south side of Business 40. Of all the businesses in the putative research park, it was clearly the most incompatible, spewing great clouds of cement dust. "It was the most visible piece of property from Business 40 looking south," Pleasants said. "At first," Pleasants recalled, "we couldn't even get them to return our calls to find out who to approach." Eventually, the corporate owner of the plant was located – in Europe!

"In each instance, these were people who were perfectly happy with where they were," Pleasants said. "They had no compulsion to sell. The only logic that worked was the prospect of improving the local economy and therefore getting them more business. And the terms of our negotiations were customized for each. For the concrete plant, we had to acquire new land and build them a new concrete plant. For Greyhound, it was negotiating a way to add them to the existing (Winston-Salem Transit Authority) bus terminal downtown. To get the city and Greyhound to see eye-to-eye and coexist in that transportation center was difficult. Noland Supply was very difficult, too. They had leased out part of their property for a cell tower right after acquiring the property in the Eighties. It was a 30- or

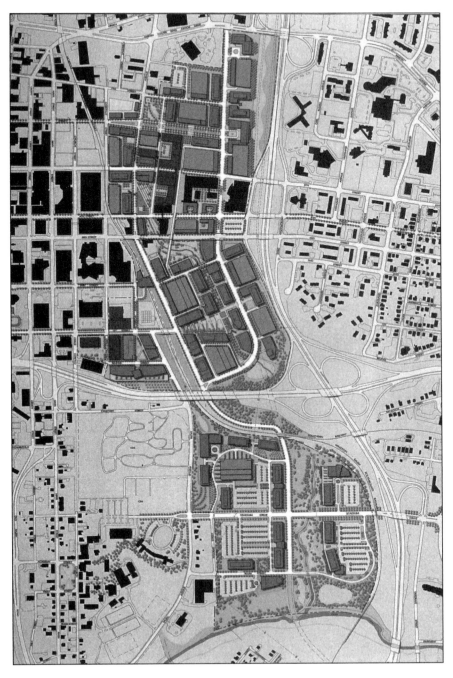

Sasaki's original master plan for the expanded research park.

40-year lease, and the cell tower was right in the middle of the central district. The negotiations started in 2002 and (10 years later) we're still talking to them. Same thing with the railroad. Our first conversation (about moving the tracks) was in August 2001, trying to get them to consider consolidating the line and negotiating all the land around it."[18]

By August 2002, negotiations with the myriad interests controlling land in the park reached the point that medical center officials felt the time was right to announce their expansion plans. Although only a small portion of the land was actually under contract, negotiations with the other landowners had reached the stage that officials felt confident that an agreement would eventually be reached. Furthermore, the medical school was celebrating its centennial during the 2002-2003 school year, and officials could think of no more fitting kick-off to the centennial than to announce the dramatic expansion. To better coordinate management of the park with the planned expansion, Dean also announced that !dealliance would be restructured as part of Wake Forest University Health Sciences, effectively turning the research park into an extension of the medical center.

Even as the medical center was basking in the overwhelmingly positive reaction to the expansion plans for the research park, a separate initiative was getting underway that would get Wake Forest Health Sciences – and with it the city's technology transformation – on the national map.

Dr. Anthony Atala had already attained international prominence for his pioneering work in growing human tissues and organs when the medical center went about recruiting him from Boston, where he was on the faculty of Harvard Medical School and the director of the Laboratory for Tissue Engineering and Cellular Therapeutics at Children's Hospital Boston. To sweeten the pot, the medical school pledged to provide Atala with an all-new research facility, custom built to his specifications – a promise that would bring the research park its next building – and the first park structure built with a specific tenant in hand. In the meantime, the medical center built out some vacant shell space in the nutrition center building for Atala's team, which arrived en masse at the end of 2003. "It was a caravan of about 20 families," Edgeton said. "They moved all at once; they drove from Boston to Winston-Salem. Talk about a brain trust coming to town."[19]

While Atala and his team went to work in the temporary quarters, the architects went to work designing a five-story, 160,000-square-foot building that would house both the newly formed Wake Forest Institute for Regenerative Medicine and the medical center's Lipid Sciences Research Program. Ground was broken for the new building on April 15, 2004, on a prominent lot at the corner of First Street and Salem Avenue, on high ground overlooking the future Central District.[20]

The promised building, called Biomedical Research Facility 1, opened in May 2006, cost $72 million, and ended up slightly larger, at 180,000 square feet. For Dick Dean, completion of the research park's new flagship building would be the last bricks-and-mortar project in the research park that he would oversee from start to finish. He retired on June 30, 2007. In recognition of his contributions to the school and the research park, Biomedical Research Facility One was renamed the Richard H. Dean Biomedical Research Building.[21]

Aerial of the research park in 2003, just after Dick Dean's plans to expand the park were unveiled. *Photo courtesy of David Rodwell*

Biomedical Research Facility 1, built specifically to house Dr. Anthony Atala's research into regenerative medicine. The building was renamed in honor of Dr. Richard Dean after his retirement.

Photo by David Rolfe, courtesy of Winston-Salem Journal

APPENDIX A:
THE WET LAB LAUNCHPAD™

Although the Dean Building, and its prestigious tenant, represented a major step forward for the research park, in some respects it was an incremental advance, because, again, the tenants for this expansion were part of the Wake Forest Baptist Medical Center. If the research park were to become the engine for a new economy in Winston-Salem, it had to become home to other high-tech companies, either by luring new tenants or growing them from scratch.

The riskier – but in some respects easier – path was to nurture start-ups arising out of promising research. But this presented the biotech equivalent of the chicken-or-egg problem: It can require very sophisticated lab facilities to commercialize a product, but typically, start-ups are not far enough down the path toward commercialization to attract the investors they need to afford these sophisticated lab facilities, which typically carried lease rates of $60 to $65 a square foot.

Everyone recognized this conundrum – and the solution. But the sheer cost of the solution was enough to keep it a hypothetical solution until 2005, when Gwen Riddick proposed what would become the Wet Lab LaunchPad™.[1]

Riddick had arrived in Winston-Salem in September 2003, to serve as the regional director for the first satellite office of the N.C. Biotechnology Center. The center, initially a component of the N.C. Commerce Department, was spun out as a stand-alone, state-funded non-profit organization in 1984 as the nation's first statewide entity dedicated to fostering biotechnology and life-science companies; successfully lobbying the state to establish the center's first satellite office in Winston-Salem was both a coup and a vote of confidence in the city's technology

157

vision. Officially, however, the office carried the more neutral designation as the "Piedmont Triad office." [2,3]

As regional director, Riddick's mandate was to promote biotechnology as a tool for growing the Triad's economy. Shortly after getting the regional office up and running, Riddick put together an advisory committee that brainstormed ideas for how it could best accomplish its mission. Out of those meetings came four priorities for promoting economic development: a recruiting quick-response package, a welcoming committee for prospects, an international incubator, and "a wet lab hotel."[4]

The last of these items would address the high cost of the specially equipped wet labs that biotech companies typically needed to pursue their research. As initially envisioned by the advisory committee, the wet lab hotel would provide low-cost facilities for medical-center spin-offs in their very early stages where they could get their footing and prove their research principles. Such space was not available anywhere in the Piedmont Triad, and existed in very limited supply elsewhere in the state.[5]

To pursue the wet lab hotel and the other economic development priorities, Riddick spent the early months of 2005 recruiting members to serve on a new Economic Development Project Team comprising representatives of economic development agencies, financial institutions, and design and contracting firms that had been active in the park or otherwise possessed the requisite abilities. James Seramba of UBS Financial Services Inc. and Randy Pool of Stantec Consulting served as co-chairs.[6]

Given that they had no site for a wet lab hotel and no money to build it even if they had a site, the team members initially considered the wet lab hotel to be a project for the mid-term. This soon changed, though, when Pool volunteered at the group's second meeting to lead the effort to create the wet lab hotel, and said that Stantec would donate the design services. Given this interest, Bill Dean suggested that there might be space in the research park for the hotel, and the committee pushed the hotel up its priority list.[7,8]

Under Pool's leadership, work on the project began in

earnest. One of the bigger challenges was determining exactly what to build. The hotel space had to be flexible enough to accommodate all types of high-tech start-ups. But cost would be a factor, and they knew they couldn't build into the flex space every type of equipment imaginable. To get a better handle on this challenge, Pool and Bill Dean spent the fall of 2005 holding a series of focus groups with park tenants, university researchers, and others. Out of those meetings came not only a better understanding of what to build, but for whom to build it. Local developers aware of the initiative were lobbying to have the space available for all biotech start-ups, not just those spun out of the medical center. As Pool explained in a letter to Bill Dean, having a facility with affordable space would help the park attract biotech entrepreneurs from outside the Triad and the state, too. "By gaining support from and establishing roots in the Triad community, the start-up firms will be more likely to remain here."[9]

An early estimate put the cost of the space at $750,000. While the group set out to start raising money, Pool began working his contacts within the construction trades to recruit a team of contractors to build the hotel when the time came. He scored an early, and vital, commitment when Kirkland Inc. agreed to serve pro bono as general contractor for the project.

Amid this progress, Riddick and the Economic Development Project Team found themselves taking a step backward when Bill Dean received a "cease and desist" letter from a rival incubator in California that had already trademarked the name "Wet Lab Hotel."[10] After culling through a new round of suggestions, the group adopted a catchy new name for their incubator that came close enough to a rhyme to give it the pizazz that "wet lab hotel" could never have conjured: "Wet Lab LaunchPad." This time, they verified that no one else had dibs on the name – and then trademarked it to keep it that way.

Even with a new name, the LaunchPad was still just an idea on paper, in that the project team still did not have a place to build it. By June 2006, the project team identified the old Dillon Supply building as a possible site. The building was just south of Third Street in the Central District and was on the market.[11] Ultimately, the team dropped the idea. The building was lacking the upscale look and feel that the project team wanted, and then it became moot when Mr. Dillon took the building off the market. The search for a location would consume the rest of the year.[12]

The impasse was finally resolved in December 2006, when Doug Edgeton formally offered to make 5,000 square feet of space in the Dean Building available for the LaunchPad – enough to provide lab and office space, and shared common areas, for three companies. Pool had started lobbying Edgeton some months before, explaining the need for the incubator and how it might ultimately become a means of creating market-rate tenants for the Dean Building or other space in the research park.[13]

With the shell space secured, the focus shifted to raising money to upfit the space. With the actual space identified, the budget was refined and came to $626,000.[14] Most of the expense would go toward the special infrastructure the facility required, starting with special plumbing that would resist the acidic and alkaline compounds that researchers use. Special ultra-low-flow flume hoods were needed to minimize the amount of air exhausted outside of the lab, and the ductwork had to be welded and fabricated with acid-resistant stainless steel. The ventilation system had to keep the lab space at negative pressure to keep fumes from migrating into the rest of the building. Even the paint on the walls had to be an epoxy formulation that would be acid-resistant and easy to clean. However, the team chose not to provide every possible amenity. Most tenants might not have need for piped gases, so permanent piping and cylinder hook-ups were not included in the upfit.

Pool teamed with Tom Ingram, Wake Forest's project manager for the research park, and Bob Radcliff of Kirkland, to raise money and recruit companies to participate in the project. The "ask" always entailed a request to have services or equipment donated, or at least discounted. The roster of those who stepped up included Salem Electric, Johnson's Modern Electric and R.L.

Vanstory, who between them donated the electrical work; Sherwin Williams, which provided the paint at cost; and Storr Office Environments, which donated the base mouldings.[15] Ultimately, the "delivery team" roster numbered 36 participants, among them AMP, Duke Energy, Graybar Electric, and Johnson Controls.[16] The number and breadth of the companies willing to participate served as a community acknowledgement that the research park – and the tilt toward technology that it represented – was becoming an important engine in the local economy.

Even with some services and equipment donated and others offered at discounted rates, the project team still faced a $250,000 shortfall. To bring the project to fruition, Bill Dean approached the city about making up half of the difference. "The timeline for completion is urgent because we have emerging life companies that need the low cost space and the private sector contributors are ready to begin construction," Dean wrote. "We will request funding consideration from Forsyth County to complete the project as well."[17] In the end, the county did not contribute, but the newly formed DataMax Corporate Foundation did.

Concurrent with the Wet Lab LaunchPad, Dean had been working to create a war chest to finance marketing efforts for the expanded research park. He had approached the foundation for a five-year marketing grant, but DataMax President Robert Egleston suggested that the foundation would be more inclined to support the LaunchPad initiative. "Our brand new foundation was all about economic development and we saw it as high-end economic development and a chance to make a difference," he said.[18]

The city's funding fell into place when the City Council approved a $125,000 forgivable loan on Aug. 20, 2007. The approval could not come soon enough for Pool. Some of the contractors and donors he had lined up for the project had been on hold for well over a year, and Pool worried that they might begin dropping by the wayside.[19] Work began the morning after the council acted, and would continue at an urgent pace. Having spent more than two years thinking about, talking about, and lining up support for the project, it would take just four months to build out the LaunchPad.

Medical center, research park, and community officials celebrated the completion of their joint effort with a ribbon-cutting ceremony on Dec. 17, 2007.[20]

The initial tenants were Tengion, a regenerative medicine company working to commercialize Atala's breakthroughs in regenerative medicine, and Carolina Liquid Chemistries, a local subsidiary of a company headquartered in California working to streamline diagnostic testing.[21]

The latter represented an immediate fulfillment of the goal of recruiting tenants from outside the local area who were not affiliated with the medical center. Company founder and president Phil Shugart, a native of Yadkinville, learned of the research park from his brother-in-law while home on a family visit in 2007. He had decided to open a small office in Winston-Salem to provide a place to work during future family visits and contacted Bill Dean about space in the research park.[22]

Although Shugart was not in the market for lab space, Dean mentioned the LaunchPad as part of his presentation about the park. After thinking things through, Shugart decided that lab space would enable the company to better serve its East Coast clients. The company started with one employee and then hired several others before moving out of the LaunchPad into a bigger space in the park, thus validating the LaunchPad's founding premise.[23]

APPENDIX B:
BUILDING THE BIOTECH WORKFORCE

In the fall of 2000, Gary Green was in his office at Calhoun Community College in Huntsville, Ala., when he received a telephone call from an executive search firm representing a community college looking for a new president.

As the leader of a tech-savvy institution with a satellite campus in the nationally recognized Cummings Research Park, Green had received such calls before. Every previous time, Green had made a few inquiries and quickly decided to stay put. But he knew that this opportunity – to lead Forsyth Technical Community College – merited more than a quick look.

"I knew Bill Dean was running the research park in Winston-Salem," Green said. "We had worked together in Huntsville when Bill was running Cummings before coming here.... So I contacted Bill and we had a conversation about what was going on in Winston-Salem and catching up.

"Huntsville was very much a high-tech and science-driven economy. While the technology (focus in Winston-Salem) was different, working in that kind of community was not new to Bill coming here or to me....

"As it turned out, one of the members of the Forsyth Tech Board of Trustees lived next door to Bill, so they had a conversation – unbeknownst to me – about me and the work that Bill and I and others had done in the Hunstville area."[1]

Six months later Green had moved into Forsyth Tech's president's office and was making the rounds in Winston-Salem to introduce himself. "A couple of things became apparent. One was Winston-Salem was going through a traumatic economic change with the decline of its legacy industries and the legacy jobs in tobacco and textiles and furniture.

"But I recall a specific meeting with Dr. Richard Dean, then the president of Wake Forest Health Sciences, and learning about their plans to expand the medical research and bio-science work that was going on.

"And Dr. Dean told me that he felt that he could attract world-class medical researchers and grow Wake Forest's position according to the standard measures of success, such as NIH funding. But there were some issues he was dealing with, and one was, where would he find the technicians to support these research functions?

"So that became part of the community college's role, to provide the technicians that would undergird the work that was in the offing in Health Sciences." Soon the college began putting together the program that would make Forsyth Tech a national leader in biotech education and make it an integral part of Winston-Salem's technological transformation.

The foundation for this shift had been laid by Green's predecessor, Desna Wallin, who arrived in 1995 as the push for technology was spreading out to the community at large.

"When I was named president," Wallin said, "my challenge, and my charge from the (Forsyth Tech) board, was to make Forsyth Tech a part of the community; to do the outreach to business, industry, and higher education to make sure we had a seat at the table. Because we did have a lot to contribute and had not been out in the community. We had stayed on our campus doing our own thing."[2]

But the college would be of limited help unless it updated its classroom technology, all of which dated to the 1980s or before. So as a crucial first step, Wallin reactivated the college's foundation in 1997 and converted it to a 501(c)3 entity that could receive donations and raise money for scholarships and technology.[3]

"This was a time when computer-aided design and manu-facturing – CAD and CAM – and statistical process control was big and new and business was looking for us to provide the training for that...and that was very costly. But we didn't have the resources we needed and we didn't have the state funding to do that."

With the money brought in to the foundation, Forsyth Tech began updating its computer labs and adding them to its Grady Swisher Center.[4]

"Another piece of that was, in all of our programs we asked our faculty to embed some sort of technology component in their syllabus," Wallin said. "That meant our arts and sciences programs as well as our technology programs. Again, our belief was that this is where the future was for our students and their employment and the community."

Concurrent with these changes, Forsyth Tech started a Small Business Development Center and located it across the hall from the Fourth Street offices of the Winston-Salem Chamber of Commerce. "We wanted to make ourselves available to business and industry...and to be a sounding board of what was going on and the concerns of small businesses.

"The emphasis was, 'We're not going to tell you what to do; you tell us what you need.' And we'll develop programs to provide what was needed."[5]

As a result of all of these actions, by the time that Green arrived as Wallin's successor, it was a given that Forsyth Tech would have a role to play in the city's technology evolution.

Before 2001 was out, Forsyth Tech would be well into developing an associate's degree in biotechnology. "We built it on the curricular strengths the college had in biology, chemistry, mathematics, and indirectly on our clinical health programs" that trained nurses and other health-field technicians, Green said.

To ensure that the program would match up well with the jobs that were being created in the research park, the school worked closely with officials at the medical center, in particular, Dr. Steve Mizel in Microbiology and Immunology; and Dr. Jim Smith in Physiology and Pharmacology.[6]

The program formally began enrolling students in the fall of 2002. It quickly grew into the largest biotechnology associate's degree program in North Carolina, with 129 students enrolled by 2005,[7] in part thanks to a serendipitous turn of events that started when U.S. Rep. Richard Burr brought Emily DeRocco, an assistant U.S. secretary of labor, to North Carolina in May 2002 for a brainstorming meeting with area leaders. They met at Shelton Vineyards in Surry County.[8] "Labor's interests were the same as ours," Green said. "They were seeing areas losing jobs and with serious unemployment levels.

"Out of that came a side discussion that day with Assistant Secretary DeRocco about what the Department of Labor was doing in skilled jobs. As it happened, they were trying to figure out what to do about biotech and how to support job creation in that area, and how to broadly develop job skills for the biotech sector. So our interests and needs in this community intersected with theirs."

That discussion led to further meetings in Washington with DeRocco, with the goal of tapping into President Bush's planned High Growth Job Training Initiative, a program on the drawing boards that was intended to prepare workers for new job opportunities in high growth sectors of the U.S. economy.[9,10]

One result of that meeting was a grant to help underwrite the cost of new equipment needed for the school's still-new biotechnology program. "That jump-started the program by providing us with the primary equipment and technology we needed in what was a high-cost program," Green said. "So we were able to grow that program fairly quickly." With this success, Forsyth Tech became part of a statewide training initiative called BioNetwork. "It was an effort in the North Carolina community college system to grow training in biotech, and we became one of five state centers for biotech training," Green said. "We were chosen because we had the largest program and had the capacity to have a leadership role." Forsyth Tech and the chamber joined forces to successfully lobby to have the network's Triad office located in the research park in 2004.[11]

But a more significant affirmation of Forsyth Tech's leadership would soon follow, when the U.S. Labor Department named Forsyth Tech to lead a new, nationwide initiative to train biotech workers.

The center was a component of the Bush Administration's newly unveiled High Growth Job Training Initiative. "We had continued our work with the Department of Labor and we had become identified as a success story for the department's Employment Training Administration," Green said, when the department issued a request for proposals to create the center as part of the overall job training initiative.

Forsyth Tech decided to pursue the opportunity and, strategically, reached out to other community colleges across the nation to create a balanced and diversified proposal. "We looked for geographic distribution," Green said, "and we looked at where the strongest regions and the strongest communities were in biotech."

Out of those conversations Forsyth Tech put together a consortium of five community colleges: Miracosta Community College in San Diego, CA; Bellevue Community College in Seattle, WA; Indian Hills Community College in Ottumwa, IA; New Hampshire Technical College in Concord, NH; and itself. "It was very deliberate geographical distribution and making sure the various sectors of biotechnology would be represented," Green said.

Forsyth Tech would focus on biotech research and development; New Hampshire Tech would concentrate on biomanufacturing; Indian Hills, capitalizing on the presence of Cargill and other big Ag companies, would emphasize agriculture and food processing; Bellevue Community College would tap into Microsoft's presence to provide training in bioinformatics; and Miracosta would highlight bioprocessing.[12]

"So we represented different regions geographically, and different sectors in biotech, and this was looked on positively by Labor," Green said. On June 28, 2004, U.S. Labor Secretary Elaine L. Chao stood in the lobby of Research One (at that point more commonly referred to as the Targacept Building) to announce a $5 million grant to Forsyth Tech and its partners to establish the National Center for the Biotechnology Workforce, with Forsyth Tech as the lead institution.[13]

The center's goal would be to develop curricula and training models for biotechnology workers, Chao said. "President Bush and I are committed to helping workers get the training they need to develop careers in growing fields like biotechnology,"

Chao said. "Through this center, training components will be developed for all major segments of the high-growth biotech sector."[14]

The grant was a one-time funding shot to get the center up and running, but Forsyth Tech was able to sustain its work through other opportunities with similar goals: initially, the state's BioNetwork program, and then a program supported by the U.S. Labor Department for a collaboration between Forsyth Tech and 10 other community colleges across the United States to disseminate best practices in biotech education. That initiative is called the Consortium for Community College Biotech Education.[15]

Concurrent with these national efforts, Forsyth Tech remained focused on its local mission of training biotech workers, and by 2006 it was averaging 25 graduates a year in its biotechnology associate's degree program.[16]

"They are lab technicians and research technicians," Green said, "working in some cases for Wake Forest medical school and health sciences in the research park and in other facilities, working for private-sector firms where they need one or two techs. They are providing exactly what we planned."

These two concurrent roles – the national and the local – merged in December 2010 when President Obama came to Forsyth Tech to draw attention to its ongoing work in training the next generation of workers. During a visit to one of the biotech labs he struck up a conversation with Kathy Proctor, a 55-year-old woman who had spent more than 30 years surviving a series of layoffs in the furniture industry. After another layoff in 2009 Proctor decided that it was time to chart a new course and enrolled in Forsyth Tech to complete the college degree she had started a few years before. She ended up in the biotech program because, she said, "I like working with my hands. And it's a growing field."[17]

Sources and Notes

Abbreviations

DDC: Downtown Development Corp.
FJB: Fowler Jones Beers
GN&R: Greensboro News & Record
HSG: Hammer, Siler, George
Int: Interview
NCBC: North Carolina Biotechnology Center
N&O: Raleigh News & Observer
PTRP: Piedmont Triad Research Park
RFP: Request for Proposals
ROD: Register of Deeds
RTP: Research Triangle Park
WFU: Wake Forest University
WSJ: Winston-Salem Journal

Prologue

1. David Fishel memo to Ron Sustana, 19 Aug 1982.
http://legacy.library.ucsf.edu/tid/ fas69d00/pdf accessed from the World Wide
Web 20 Aug 2008.
2. RJR Tobacco website – Tobaccoville manufacturing center; Fishel memo.
3. RJR Reynolds Monthly briefing, October 1982.
http://legacy.library.ucsf.edu.8080/w/x/s/wxs49d00/Swxs49d00.pdf accessed from
the World Wide Web 20 Aug. 20 2008.
4. Fishel memo
5. ibid
6. Interview with Gayle Anderson 10 Aug 2006
7. ibid.

Chapter 1: The Rise and Fall of Camel City

1. Frank V. Tursi, Susan White and Steve McQuilkin, "Lost Empire: The Fall
of R.J. Reynolds Tobacco Co.," 2000, Winston-Salem Journal, Winston-
Salem, N.C. p. 262
2. ibid, p. 267

3. Interview with Jerry Long, 1 Nov 2006
4. Tursi et al, p. 261
5. James Howell Smith, Winston-Salem in History, Vol. 8 Industry and Commerce 1896-1975 Monograph
6. ibid
7. ibid p. 44-45
8. Tursi et al, p. 265
9. ibid, pp. 262-263
10. Inman etc: Tursi et al p. 262-264
11. Long int.
12. ibid
13. Tursi et al, p. 301
14. WSJ 8 March 1959
15. WSJ 15 Jan 1986
16. Frank Elliott, "Piedmont: Flight of the Pacemaker," 2007, Piedmont Aviation Historical Society, Winston-Salem N.C.
17. WSJ 21 Jan 1988
18. Tursi et al, p. 307
19. WSJ 11 Aug 1989
20. WSJ 7 April 1989

Chapter 2: False Starts

1. Interview with Gayle Anderson 10 Aug 2006
2. Interview with Douglas Maynard 4 Dec 2008
3. Maynard memo, "Ideas for ERC" 11 Jul 1985
4. Maynard int.
5. Interview with Richard Janeway 21 Mar 2008
6. Maynard memo, 10 Jun 1986
7. Maynard memo "Information from VPI Visit," 5 July 1988
8. ibid
9. Janeway int.
10. ibid
11. Maynard letter to Robert Emken, 27 July 1988
12. ibid
13. Maynard letter to John Anderson, 3 Aug 1988
14. Anderson memo to Tom Hearn 10 Nov 1988
15. RJR Tobacco Co. Community Relations Survey March 1989
16. Maynard memo to Janeway, 17 Feb 1989
17. Maynard letter to Jerry Long, 21 Apr 1989
18. ibid;, dollar figure from Maynard letter to Zack Smith 9 May 1989
19. Long letter
20. Smith letter
21. Maynard served as vice chair of technology, a recently created position

to coordinate the engineering initiative and other technology-related opportunities.

22. Maynard letter to Gayle Anderson 17 Jul 1989
23. ibid
24. Interview with Gayle Anderson 15 Oct 2008
25. Leon Corbett memo to Hearn, 2 Oct 1989
26. ibid
27. The committee also comprised John Boehme, Pete Santago, Dick Witcofski, Hank Chilton, Dixon Moody, Wes Snyder, Joanne Ruhland, Hof Milam
28. Confidential Report on Graduate Engineering, May 1990
29. Maynard int.
30. Maynard memo to Hearn et al 2 Jan 1991
31. Interview with Pete Santago 10 Mar 2008
32. Maynard memo 2 Jan 1991
33. ibid
34. David G. Brown letter to Maynard 11 Dec 1990
35. Maynard letter 14 Feb 1991
36. Maynard memo 25 Mar 1991
37. Maynard memo 19 April 1991
38. Draft bill
39. Maynard ltr 24 Jun 91

Chapter 3. Operation Pinetree

1. WSJ 12 Nov 1991
2. Gayle Anderson e-mail, 29 Apr 2015
3. 15 years later, Maynard would say of his scatter shot thinking on a research park: "We were determined to do something. We'd open any door we could to try to do something." (Maynard int)
4. Technology Committee Operation Pinetree presentation dated 6 Sep 1991
5. ibid
6. ibid
7. ibid
8. WSJ 10 Nov 1991
9. Interview with Gayle Anderson, 23 Dec 2008
10. ibid
11. HSG report dated 7 May 1992, p.1
12. ibid p. 2
13. ibid pp.4-5
14. Congress first appropriated nearly $3 million for the Center for Research on Human Nutrition and Chronic Disease Prevention in 1989. Shortly thereafter, however, the federal government reduced spending on projects such as the Nutrition Center, leaving the building with not nearly enough

money to be completed as scheduled. The outside shell of the 11-story, 248,000-square-foot tower was finally completed in 1996 and first completed floor of Nutrition Center opened in September, 1988. The rest of the floors were completed bit by bit as money allowed. Consequently, the Nutrition Center was slowly worked on floor by floor as they received funding bit by bit. Between the lost momentum and the slow build-out, the center never did become a stimulus for the park.
(*http://www.wakehealth.edu/Library/Archives/Buildings/1990s-at-Baptist.htm*, accessed 2 Sep 2015)

15. HSG report 7 May 1992 p.6
16. Maynard int.
17. HSG report 7 May 1992 p. 8
18. ibid pp.11-12
19. ibid p.13
20. ibid p.14
21. The research parks were Research Triangle Park; the Massachusetts Biotechnology Park in Worchester, Mass.; Northwestern University/ Evanston Research Park; Hopkins Bayview Research Campus in Baltimore; the University of Utah Research Park in Salt Lake City; University Research Park in Charlotte; Carolina Research Park in Columbia, S.C.; Clemson Research Park in Clemson, S.C.; Chicago Technology Park; and Miami Valley Research Park outside Dayton, Ohio.
22. HSG rpt. 7 May 1992 p. 23
23. ibid pp. 18,30
24. ibid p. 25
25. ibid p. 29
26. ibid p. 30
27. ibid p. 32
28. ibid p. 33
29. ibid p. 34
30. ibid p. 32
31. ibid p. 1

Chapter 4: Engineering the Triad

1. Carson report p. 5
2. ibid p. 2
3. WSJ 22 Nov 1991
4. N&O 12 Oct 1991
5. ibid
6. ibid
7. GN&R 12 Oct 1991
8. Carson report p. 5
9. GN&R 12 Oct 1991

10. WSJ 21 Oct 1991
11. ibid
12. Triad Business Journal 11 Nov 1991; N&R 12 Oct 1991
13. Carson p. 3
14. Rounding out the committee were C.C. Cameron of Charlotte, Rod Adams of Durham, and Pricilla Taylor of Greensboro. WSJ 21 Oct 1991
15. WSJ 22 Nov 1991
16. ibid
17. ibid
18. GN&R 14 Dec 1991
19. Maynard int. 24 Oct 2006
20. WSJ 15 Dec 1991
21. GN&R 15 Dec 1991
22. Carson report p. 4
23. Carson report p. 6
24. ibid
25. ibid
26. ibid
27. WSJ 23 Apr 1992

Chapter 5: A New Vision

1. Vernon George email 5 May 2015
2. ibid
3. George ltr. to Gayle Anderson 17 Jul 1989
4. Maynard int. 24 Oct 2006
5. ibid
6. HSG memo 14 May 1992
7. George email
8. Willem Hulsink and Hans Dons, "Pathways to High Tech Valleys and Research Triangles: Innovative Entrepreneurship, Knowledge Transfer and Cluster Formation in Europe and the United States" Springer, 2008 p. 46-47
9. ibid p. 41
10. ibid p. 44
11. ibid
12. In the early years, RTP's remote location was detrimental in efforts to market the park. It took the national clout of Gov. Terry Sanford within Democratic circles to get the Johnson administration to commit to putting the HEW facility in the park, which paved the way for IBM to follow. George email 5 May 2015
13. Michael I. Lugar and Harvey A. Goldstein, "Technology in the Garden: Research Parks and Regional Economic Development," 1991, University of North Carolina Press, Chapel Hill p. 5
14. ibid

15. HSG memo 14 May 1992

16. ibid

17. ibid

18. ibid

19. ibid

20. Maynard letter to Steven Hassenfelt 5 Oct 1992

21. ibid

22. Haver RFP, 1 Oct 92

23. WSJ 27 Feb 1994

24. Nannie Tilley, "The R.J. Reynolds Tobacco Co.," 1985, University of North Carolina Press, pp 516-517. Reynolds originally used the building to research more efficient use of tobacco leaf. Later research efforts focused on the chemistry of tobacco after links between tobacco use and cancer began to surface.

25. Haver RFP, 1 Oct 1992; the square footage totals include an expansion of the building in 1954

26. ibid

27. WSJ 27 Feb 1994

28. Janeway letter to RJR Tob. Co. 23 Nov 1992

29. ibid

30. ibid

31. ibid

32. HSG report January 1993 pp. 51-52

33. ibid pp.53, 55

34. ibid p. 55

35. ibid p. 56

36. HSG report. Appendix

37. ibid pp. 63, 60

38. ibid pp. 56, 57, 64

39. ibid Table 7

40. ibid p. 65

41. ibid pp. 53-54

42. Maynard int. 24 Oct 2006

43. George email

Chapter 6. The Jailhouse Campus

1. Santago letter to Harold Martin 7 Dec 1992

2. ibid

3. ibid

4. Maynard memo 21 Oct 1992

5. ibid

6. ibid

7. Santago letter 7 Dec 1992

8. Maynard memo to Tom Hearn 26 Mar 1993

9. Anderson letter to John McNair 13 Apr 1993. Lest the UNC Board of Governors get the wrong impression, Anderson sent a letter to each member of the board, explaining this strategy with the assurance that Winston-Salem was committed to operating the engineering center "as the Carson committee and the UNC Board of Governors has structured it."

10. Maynard memo 26 March 1993

11. WSJ 9 May 1993

12. Interview with Richard Janeway 21 Mar 2008

13. Janeway int.

14. Interview with Jim Smith 5 Dec 2006

15. ibid

16. ibid

17. ibid

18. ibid

19. ibid

20. As it would turn out, two faculty members, fearful of being isolated in the downtown building, chose to stay on the Hawthorne campus.

21. Smith int.

22. Interview with Cleon Thompson, 10 Aug 2006

23. Interview with Ted Kaplan, 31 July 2006

24. Kaplan int. & SB 26, 1993 session

25. Maynard int.

26. Thompson int.

27. Maynard memo15 Sep 1993

28. Maynard letter to Cleon Thompson 8 Oct 1993

29. ibid

30. WSJ 27 Feb 1994

31. ibid. Despite the PR flap, Winston-Salem officials maintained a cordial working relationship with Memory insofar as PTERC fell under his purview within the university system.

Chapter 7: If You Build It, Will They Come?

1. WSJ 9 Nov 1994

2. ibid

3. Maynard memo 12 Aug 1994

4. ibid

5. Interview with Jack Steelman 19 Oct 2010

6. Maynard memo 12 Aug 1994

7. PTRP Management committee minutes 5 Aug 1994

8. ibid

9. ibid

10. Vernon George memo to Doug Maynard 27 Oct 1994

11. Although the census identified a number of prospects, no substantive prospects emerged and the effort, though worthy, came to naught.

12. Frank Elliott, Wake Forest magazine, June 1999

13. ibid

14. ibid

15. Southeastern Institute of Research Inc. "Potential Adaptive Re-Uses for R.J. Reynolds Buildings," research report to Forsyth County 29 Dec 1992

16. Tilley, p. 68-69

17. ibid

18. Appraisal by Michael D. Avent & Associates 6 Sep 1994

19. Interview with Jerry Long, 1 Nov 2006

20. Avent appraisal; closing documents

21. Appraisal by Michael D. Avent & Associates 15 Sep 1994. The Downtown Development Corp. bought the property on 29 Apr 1995. Closing documents; Forsyth County ROD Book 1856 p.2315

22. Appraisal by Michael D. Avent & Associates 7 Sep 1994; Ken Blackburn letter to Jack Steelman 11 Nov 1994; bought 12 May 1995 ROD Book 1857 pg. 855

23. Piedmont Triad Research Park Master Plan Exec Summary, Jan 1995

24. Curry letter to Jack Steelman 21 Jul 1994

25. Master plan

26. ibid

27. DDC files

28. Closing documents, ROD book 1886 p. l851

29. ibid

30. DDC files

31. Steelman int.

32. ibid

33. ibid

34. Details of the deal are found in the DDC files.

35. WSJ 16 Dec 1996 p. B7. Shannon had met Jon Wilson through Bill Todd of Todd Motion Controls, another tenant he was courting. (Shannon e-mail 2 Dec. 32015)

36. Wiltek's lease was put up as part of the collateral for the loan. (Closing documents)

37. Minutes of Forsyth County Commissioners, 13 May 1996

38. Closing documents dated 14 Jun 1996) As structured, Wolf Pond committed to redeveloping 256-9 as phase 1 of the project. The estimated cost for redeveloping the entire Building 256 complex carried an estimated price tag of $2.024 million. (CCB letter to JDL Castle Corp. dated 8 May 1996, included in closing documents.)

Chapter 8: When the Going Gets Tough...

1. Interview with Pete Santago 10 Mar 2008
2. Wall Street Journal, 14 Feb 1996. The Winston-Salem Journal carried a wire report on the Wall Street Journal story in its Jan. 15 edition. As a consolation to local boosters, the wire report noted that the Triad managed to eke out a job-growth rate "barely above the national average," thanks to its favorable location midway between Atlanta and Washington D.C. "and a surging service sector, led by a nationally ranked medical-research and treatment center in Winston-Salem."
3. Chamber Technology Council proposal, March 1996
4. ibid
5. ibid
6. Chamber powerpoint presentation"Technology Economic Development" dated 20 Dec 1996
7. ibid
8. Maynard community presentation on Technology Initiative, 5 Jan. 1998
9. Maynard int. 24 Oct 2006
10. Maynard community presentation on Technology Initiative, 5 Jan. 98
11. Maynard int.
12. WSJ 25 Apr 1997 p. D1
13. PTRP presentation
14. PTRP memorandum of understanding between DDC, City of Winston-Salem, Winston-Salem Chamber of Commerce and Winston-Salem Business Inc. 1 Sep 1996
15. ibid
16. The expo carried the cumbersome and somewhat amorphous name "Connectivity: The Winston-Salem Research and Technology Vision." (WSJ 16 Dec 1996 p. B1)
17. WSJ 16 Dec 1996 p. B7
18. Brice Shearburn (JDC Castle) memo to Brooke Wozniak (DDC) 30 Jan 1998
19. Steelman memo to David Park and Fred Nordenholz 2 May 1997
20. FJB Research One Proposal 5 Jun 1996
21. ibid
22. Draft Development Agreement, Research Park Speculative Research Building, July 1996
23. Joines memo to Steve Johnson (FJB) 30 July 1996
24. Joines memo to DDC Executive Committee, 31 Jul 1996
25. Nordenholz memo to Joines 5 Aug 1996
26. "Forsyth County's Blueprint for Technology Development, December 1997
27. ibid
28. ibid

29. ibid
30. ibid
31. Maynard int.
32. Maynard comments 19 Nov. 2015
33. The recap of this meeting is drawn from Doug Maynard's prepared remarks at the event.
34. Maynard int.
35. Maynard memo to Tom Hearn 19 March, 1998. The inaugural committee members were: Chairman: Thomas Hearn, President, Wake Forest University. Vice-Chairmen: Bud Baker, CEO, Wachovia Corp.; Andy Schindler, CEO, R.J. Reynolds Tobacco Co. Members: John Allison, CEO, Branch Banking & Trust; Kirk Beaudin, CEO, Sara Lee Knit Products; Richard Brenner, President, Amarr Co.; Wendy Burden, General Manager, Pepsi-Cola Customer Service Center; Nancy Dunn, President, Aladdin Travel; Charlie Federico, President, Orthofix Inc.; Vic Flow, Flow Automotive Cos.; Rob Greene, Manager, Administrative Services, BB&T; Jim Lambie, Chairman, BizNexus; Jerry Long; L.A. Reynolds Home & Garden Showplace; Walter McDowell, CEO, Wachovia Bank of North Carolina; John McKinnon, Management Consultant; John Millican, Vice President, Salem Computer Group; Glenn Orr, President, Orr Management Co.; Len Preslar, CEO, N.C. Baptist Hospital; Jack Ward, President, J.F. Ward Group; John Whitaker, Chairman, Inmar Enterprises; Paul Wiles, President, Novant Health; Tab Williams, Chairman, Williams Oil Co.; Murray Greason, Partner, Womble Carlyle Sandridge & Rice; George Little, Partner, Kilpatrick Stockton; Richard Dean, Senior Vice President for Health Affairs, WFU School of Medicine; Alex Ewing, Chancellor, NC School of the Arts; Alvin Schnexnider, Chancellor, Winston-Salem State University; Julianne Thrift, President, Salem College & Academy; Desna Wallin, President, Forsyth Technical Community College. Ex-Officio: Rep. Richard Burr, John Anderson, Vice President Finance & Administration, WFU; John Boehme; James Bullock; Doug Maynard; Jay Moskowitz; Charles Moyer; Jerry Long, chairman of the Chamber of Commerce; Rence Callahan, chairman of the Downtown Development Corp.; Kirk Glenn, chairman of Winston-Salem Business Inc.
36. Hearn memo to executive committee 18 Mar 1998. The executive committee was Hearn, Bud Baker, Andy Schindler, Nancy Dunn, Rob Greene, Walter McDowell, John McKinnon, Murray Greason, Richard Dean, Alvin Schnexnider, John Anderson, James Bullock and Doug Maynard
37. The planning committee was chaired by Doug Maynard and comprised Gayle Anderson; John Anderson; Russell Armistead, Assoc. Dean, Administrative Services WFU School of Medicine; Donald deBethizy, Vice President, Product Evaluation, R&D, R.J. Reynolds Tobacco; Charles Moyer, Dean of WFU Babcock School of Management; Jay Moskowitz, Assoc. Dean, Office of Research Development, WFU School of Medicine; Tim Rice, Executive Vice President, BB&T; Walter McDowell; and John McKinnon.

(Maynard memo to committee members 16 Jan 1998)

38. Maynard memo to committee members 16 Jan 1998
39. ibid
40. WFU Technology Transfer and Business Development Plan 16 Dec 1997
41. ibid
42. ibid
43. ibid
44. Hearn memo to NCETA board 14 April 1998; minutes of meeting
45. ibid

Chapter 9: Getting Serious

1. Interview with Bill Dean, l4 Dec 2006
2. ibid
3. ibid
4. 1995-96 Worldwide Research Science Park Directory, published by Assoc of University Related Research Parks
5. Dean int.
6. ibid
7. ibid
8. NCETA Executive Committee minutes, 22 Jun 1998
9. Interview with Jack Steelman 19 Oct 2010
10. Hearn memo to NCETA board, 24 June 1998. Joines also believed that construction of the hotel and the city office building would encourage development in the park (Jones e-mail 15 Dec 2015)
11. Interview with Jim Capps, 29 Aug 2010
12. Memo to Jeff Greg Frisby from Brice Shearburn of JDL Castle, 22 Oct 1996
13. JDL Castle draft news release March 1998
14. Steelman int.
15. WSJ 9 Sep 1998
16. Capps int.
17. WSJ 9 Sep 1998 & 28 Aug 1998
18. ibid
19. Frank Elliott, Wake Forest magazine, June 1999
20. Wall Street Journal, January, 1999
21. Capps int.
22. Account of fire drawn from stories published in WSJ and N&O Aug 28 & 29, 1998
23. Tilley, The R.J. Reynolds Tobacco Co. p. 69. UNC Press, 1985
24. Steelman int
25. WSJ 28 Aug 1998
26. Steelman memo to NCETA board, 3 Sep 1998)
27. WSJ 28 Aug 1998

28. Frisby eventually declared bankruptcy in 2002 WSJ 20 Feb 03

29. Steelman memo to NCETA board, 3 Sep 1998

30. WSJ 28 Aug 1998

31. Hearn memoto NCETA board members, 23 Sep 1998

32. ibid

33. NCETA minutes of meeting 16 0ct 1998; Hearn memo to NCETA board members 10 Dec 1998. In the end, the offer was moot because the building did not include any spec wet lab space.

34. Lloyd Whittington, The Business Journal, 22 Jan 1999

35. WSJ 6 Jan 1999

36. NCETA Executive Committee minutes 11 Feb 1999; Hearn memo to NCETA board members Mar 1998

37. Dean int.

38. ibid

39. ibid

40. ibid

Chapter 10: Technology for All

1. Ellen Dockham Wake Forest magazine,June 1999

2. Interview with John Boehme, 27 Apr 2012

3. T-1 lines are direct connections between points on a network that can carry multiple signals. At the time, T-1 lines used copper wire and had limited capacity to carry data.

4. Boehme int.

5. ibid

6. Hearn memos to NCETA board, 24 Jun 1998 and 1 Mar 1999

7. As the process developed Wake Forest modified its fiber routes to bring them as close as possible, without undue cost, to the participating institutions so that when each institution went forward with the connection it would be as easy and inexpensive as possible. For example, the hand-hold for Winston-Salem State was installed at the intersection of Technology Way and Salem Avenue. (Boehme email to Gayle Anderson 10Apr 2015)

8. Boehme int.

9. It's not exactly clear when the fiber network came to be known as WinstonNet. There was no formal process of naming it, Boehme said, rather, he started referring to the project as WinstonNet and the name caught on. Forsyth County Manager Graham Perview later lamented, in good humor, that it was not called "ForsythNet," but, Boehme said, "It just did not have the same ring.... We challenged that and thought about it, but we kept coming back to 'WinstonNet' "(Boehme int. and email to Gayle Anderson 28 Apr 15)

10. Wake Forest University's early leadership in developing a community network paid dividends when MCNC invited it to be one of the founding

institutions participating in Internet 2, a parallel internet connection to MCNC reserved for educational and research institutions. Internet 2 gives Wake a faster connection to the internet because it is not competing with all the commercial connections. (Boehme int.)

11. The Winston-Salem Chamber's Technology Committee had approached the school system about hiring a consultant out of recognition that shifting the city to a technology-oriented economy would require technology-savvy workers. With the agreement of the school system, the chamber helped finance the study. Anderson int)

12. Strategic Technology Plan for Winston-Salem/Forsyth County Schools, Barry/Levinston Enterprise, Washington D.C. dated Feb. 15, 1998

13. ibid p. 12

14. ibid p. 16

15. ibid p. 25

16. ibid p. 63

17. ibid p. 20

18. ibid p. 23

19. ibid p. 16

20. Interview with Gayle Anderson 10 Aug 2006

21. Triad Business Journal 6 Feb 2003

22. Interview with Bill Dean 14 Dec 2006

23. ibid

24. Interview with Don DeBethizy, 27 Dec 2010

25. ibid

26. Dean int.

27. DeBethizy int.

28. Piedmont Triad Business, a special publication of Piedmont Triad Partnership, undated

29. WSJ, 28 Sep 2001

30. Dean int.

31. ibid

32. ibid

33. ibid

34. JDL Castle release 7 Apr 2000

Chapter 11: Rebooting

1. Interview with Pete Santago, 10 Mar 2008

2. ibid; the episode Santago refers to with Jasper Memory is recounted in Chapter 6.

3. Santago private notes on PTERC

4. Santago int.

5. ibid

6. ibid

7. The Virginia Tech - Wake Forest School of Biomedical Engineering and Sciences Executive Study, 15 March 2001

8. ibid

9. ibid

10. ibid

11. The 13 departments were Anesthesiology, Internal Medicine, Medical Engineering, Neurology, Pediatrics, Radiology, Cardiothoracic Surgery, General Surgery, Neurosurgery, Opthamology, Orthopaedics, Plastic and Reconstructive Surgery, and Urology.

12. The Virginia Tech - Wake Forest School of Biomedical Engineering and Sciences Executive Study, 15 March 2001

13. Memorandum of Understanding between the two universities, 21 Dec 2001

14. Santago int.

15. The Virginia Tech - Wake Forest School of Biomedical Engineering and Sciences Executive Study, 15 March 2001

16. Santago int.

17. ibid

18. WFU release 19 Mar 2003

19. Maynard memo to Richard Dean, 4 Nov 2002

20. WFU release 28Mar 2003

21. Santago int.

22. Maynard memo to Richard Dean, 4 Nov 2002

23. Santago int.

24. ibid

25. Email from Dr. Stefan Duma, 4 Mar 2016. Faculty working with the program also soared, from 10 in 2003 to 85 in 2016, while while sponsored research grew from $1 million in 2003 to $30 million in 2016.

Epilogue

1. Interview with Dick Dean 30 Sep 2015; WFU news release 13 Aug. 2002

2. "Star Wars theme: The Business Journal, Aug 13, 2002.

3. WFU news release 13 Aug. 2002

4. The Business Journal, Aug 13, 2002

5. WSJ 8 Apr 2003

6. The Medical Center cracked the top-40 in 2001, when it pulled in $90.3 million in NIH-sponsored research, ranking it 36th. (WFU news release 3 Mar 2002) In 2005 it would set a new high with $128.7 million in NIH funding, putting it in 32nd overall among American medical schools. (WFU news release 24 Jun 2005)

7. Interview with Graydon Pleasants, 10 May 2012

8. ibid

9. Dean int.

10. Gayle Anderson e-mail to author 14 Apr 2014

11. Winston-Salem Tobacco Historic District, National Register of Historic Places Registration Form, July 29, 2008; revised March 30, 2009. N.C. State Historic Preservation Office.

12. Dean int.

13. Pleasants int.

14. Interview with Doug Edgeton 12 Apr 2012

15. Edgeton int.

16. Sasaki devised a plan that called for dividing the expanded park into three distinct districts, North, Central and South. The medical center's research campus – the original raison d'etre for the expansion, would occupy the Central District, immediately east of, and adjoining, the existing park, and the master plan correspondingly went into much more detail for its development.

Here, the master plan envisioned a fairly dense mix of three- and four-story buildings in a "pedestrian-oriented" campus totalling almost 1.3 million square feet, to be developed in five phases. Five accompanying parking decks for 4,000 cars would be tucked to the rear, out of the prime sightlines within the district. Although distinctly urban in feel, the master plan called for opening Town Creek, which was buried in a culvert running through the site, to provide an attractive linear green space and water feature. What railroad sidings remained from the tract's earlier use as a railroad yard would be removed and the through railroad line, still in use, would be shifted to the western edge. An old wooden railroad trestle would be converted to an elevated service road over Third Street, which marked the division between the central and north districts.

The north district would be a "mixed-use village" of private tech-related companies, apartments and condos and supporting retail businesses, such as restaurants. The downtown street network between Third and Eighth streets on the west side would be extended into the North District to better integrate it into downtown. The existing Reynolds factories would be retained, along with Wachovia's new Linden Street center and two historic structures: Piedmont Leaf Lofts and the Nissen Wagon Works.

The south district would be a less-dense collection of buildings and surface parking lots serving private tenants as well as Winston-Salem State University and Salem College. Green space would be provided by a 300-foot wide park and greenway that would cut from north to south through the district along the banks of Cloverleaf Branch, a tributary to Salem Creek.

17. Pleasants int.

18. ibid

19. Edgeton int.

20. WFU news release, 15 Apr 2004

21. WFU news release 30 Sep 2007

Appendix A: The Wet Lab LaunchPad

1. WFU release 12-17-07)

2. NCBC release on PR newswire, accessed 23 Apr 15
(www.prnewswire.com/news-releases/ director-hired-for-piedmont-triad-
office-of-north-carolina-biotechnology-center-70999527.html)

3. The lobbying effort was no doubt enhanced by the incentive package the
community offered, most significantly, $200,000 that Wake Forest
University Health Sciences committed over two years to staff the office with
a director and and full-time assistant. The package also included an offer
from !dealliance to provide office space, Forsyth Technical Community
College's donation of two computer workstations, and free high-speed internet access courtesy of WinstonNet. (ibid)

4. Riddick email to Randal Pool, 8 Mar 2005

5. Pool letter to Bill Dean 1 Jun 2006

6. Project Team members were Seramba, Pool, Peggy Low of the Winston-
Salem Chamber of Commerce, Don DeBethizy of Targacept, Penny
Whiteheart of the Piedmont Triad Partnership, Pricilla Taylor of Cemala
Foundation, Bill Dean of !dealliance, Jim Lanning of IBM, John Geib of
Duke Power and Tony Johnson of the Small Business & Technology
Development Center; Riddick sat as an advisor. (Project Team Minutes, 29
Jun 2005)

7. Project Team Minutes, 29 Jun 2005

8. Pool's interest in the wet lab hotel stemmed from his father, who taught
biochemistry at Winston-Salem State. Although his father's research con-
tributed to the body of knowledge in his field, Pool rued the fact that his
father and others like him were never able to gain financially from their
life's work. When he saw the wet lab hotel on the list of possible projects he
immediately saw it not only as an engine for economic development, but as
a way to create an opportunity for others that his father never had. (Pool
int. 6 Oct. 2015)

9. Pool letter to Bill Dean 1 Jun 2006

10. Pool int. 6 Oct 2015

11. Pool letter to Bill Dean 1 Jun 2006

12. Pool int.

13. ibid

14. Bill Dean letter to Derwick Paige 26 Jul 2007

15. Wet Lab LaunchPad construction meeting minutes, 21 Sep 2007

16. The full delivery team comprised AMP, Arc One, Armstrong Resource
Flooring, Carolina Business Interiors, the City of Winston-Salem, Crown
Lifts, DataMax, Duke Energy, Environmental Air Systems, Ferguson,
Gallagher-Stone, Graybar Electric, Hahn Mason Inc., Hales Insulation,
Interior Enterprizes, Johnson Controls Inc., Johnsonite, Johnsons Modern

Electric, Kewaunee, Kirkland Inc., L. Fishman Inc., Luwa, Mannington, Net Unlimited, R. L. Vanstory, Salem Electric, Sears, Shaw, Sherwin-Williams, Sloop, Snead Paint Company, Stantec, Storr Office Environments, Sunland Fire Protection Inc., The Phoenix Agency, and Wake Forest University Health Sciences (WFU news release 17 Dec. 2007)

17. Bill Dean letter to Derwick Paige 26 Jul 2007

18. Interview with Robert Egleston 8 Oct 2015. The DataMax Corporate Foundation had just been formed in the spring of 2007 with proceeds of the sale of the Retail Merchants Association, a 27-county credit bureau, to Equifax. The board voted to take the lion's share of the proceeds and put them into a foundation to put the money back to work for the benefit of the community. (Egleston int.)

19. Pool int.

20. Work on the building went up almost to the last minute. Office furniture, some shelving and breakroom equipment were not scheduled to be installed until Dec. 12, and the mechanical chases for the lab islands were to go in on Dec. 13, giving the project team only one business day to make up for delays. (LaunchPad project team minutes 10 Dec 2007)

21. WFU release 17 Dec 2007

22. Gayle Anderson interview with Phil Shugart, 1 May 2015

23. ibid

Appendix B: Building the Biotech Workforce

1. Interview with Gary Green, 12 Jan 2016

2. Interview with Desna Wallin, 11 Jan 2016

3. ibid

4. ibid

5. ibid

6. Green int.

7. FTCC Institutional Research records

8. Department of Labor news release, 6 May 2002, "Coordinated Effort Between U.S. Departments of Labor and Commerce Aids Dislocated North Carolina Workers."

9. Green int.

10. DeRocco's familiarity with FTCC's efforts to establish its biotech program no doubt played a role in the White House's decision to have President Bush visit the school in November 2003 to promote his administration's efforts to create new jobs.

11. Concurrent with this, FTCC developed an associate's degree in nanotechnology program to support the WF Institute for Nanotechnology and Molecular Materials, created in 2003 by acquiring David Carroll's research group at Clemson University.

12. Green int.

13. Department of Labor news release, 28 Jun 2004, "Labor Secretary Chao Announces $5M Biotechnology Grant to Forsyth Technical Community College, Partners." The overall budget for the High Growth initiative was $17.2 million

14. ibid

15. Green int.

16. FTCC Institutional Research records

17. *https://www.forsythtech.edu/president-obama/meet-kathy-proctor/Meet Kathy Proctor*, retrieved Jan. 14, 2016